CHRISTIAN MICROENTERPRISE DEVELOPMENT

An Introduction

CHRISTIAN MICROENTERPRISE DEVELOPMENT

An Introduction

David Bussau and Russell Mask

A project of Christian Transformation Resource Center
An Activity of CMED Network and Infemit

regnum

First published 2003 by Regnum Books International
in association with
Paternoster Press, 9 Holdom Avenue, Bletchley, Milton Keynes MK1 1QR, UK
and PO Box 1047, Waynesboro, GA 30830–2047, USA

Reprinted, 2005

Regnum Books International is a Two-Thirds World publishing company for the International
Fellowship of Evangelical Mission Theologians (INFEMIT), formed of the African Theological
Fellowship, the Latin American Theological Fraternity and Partnership in Mission Asia.
PO Box 70, Oxford OX2 6HB, UK
PO Box 76, Akropong-Akuapem, Ghana
Jose Marmol 1734, 1602 Florida, Buenos Aires, Argentina
Post Bag No 21, Vasant Kunj, New Delhi 110057, India
c/o Glad Sound SDN, BHD, PO Box 1019, Jalan Semangat, 46970 Petaling Jaya, Malaysia
55 Fair Drive, Costa Mesa, CA 92626, USA

09 08 07 06 05 04 03   7 6 5 4 3 2 1

British Library Cataloguing in Publication Data
A catalogue record for this book is available from the British Library.

ISBN 1-870345-28-2

Typeset by Profile, Culmdale, Rewe, Exeter,
and printed and bound in Great Britain by
Bell and Bain Ltd, Glasgow.

Contents

117862

About the Authors

David Bussau

David Bussau has a rich background in holistic development having ministered for 25 years in over 60 countries with a broad range of holistic development objectives.

He is considered the father of Christian Microenteprise Development (CMED) and has pioneered numerous creative and vibrant microenteprise development programs. His knowledge and involvement in global Christian development networks positions him to share his microenteprise development experiences to a wide audience of readers.

He has written other booklets on CMED: "Reflections on Christian Microenteprise Development" and "How then shall we lend?" In 1999, he conceptualized and organized an international conference on Christian Microenteprise Development held in Bangkok, Thailand attended by over 100 organizations.

Russell Mask

Russell Mask is the International Microenteprise Coordinator at Chalmers Center for Economic Development at Covenant College. He worked and conducted research on livelihood and MED

programs in the Philippines and Kenya for seven and a half years and is currently training Christian development workers and missionaries and via distance education. He finished his Masters in Sociology and Ph.D. in Development at the University of Wisconsin-Madison.

Preface and Acknowledgements

The past decade of the millennium has seen a resurgence of mission endeavors in countries hostile to the gospel particularly in the 10-40 window. Church growth demographers extrapolate that the church will triple over the next ten years with 3.1 million new churches started.[1] These churches will require economic engines to sustain them.

Dynamic mission groups are always searching for authentic approaches to serve communities with integrity and remain faithful to biblical scripture. Of the various approaches attempted, one in particular that has arrested the imagination and enthusiasm of many mission organizations is Microenterprise Development (MED). The emergence and success of these programs as a mainstream development strategy has captured the attention of governments, aid organizations, national churches in the 2/3 world and mission programs. Recent surveys suggest that in excess of 1200 different Christian organizations, are currently implementing MED in the 2/3 world. Sadly, most of these efforts have commenced with little understanding of the basic fundamentals of creating a credit culture with the discipline and knowledge of the best practices required.

Furthermore, the biblical validation and underpinning for capital supply, wealth creation, and the stewardship of such resources are invariably given little attention and are seldom integrated into the worldview of the organization.

In a world which increasingly dichotomises between the sacred and the secular, it is imperative that Christian Microenterprise Development

(CMED) organizations witness to a holistic gospel which does not limit God only to matters of eternity, and ascribes the solutions of poverty and deprivation to the secular specialists.

This handbook attempts to bring a perspective which will position Christian Development Organizations (CDOs) as effective purveyors of a gospel which attests to a God of redemption and transformation through holistic ministry.

The authors wish to acknowledge the support of the following Christian donor foundations without whom this Handbook would not have been produced: First Fruit Foundation, Lundman Family Foundation, Maclellan Foundation, Stewardship Foundation, Fieldstead & Co. and Maranatha Trust.

Many thanks is likewise extended to the Chalmers Center for Economic Development at Covenant College and World Relief for their generous financial contributions to its completion as well as to the research and writing of some of the cases.

This Handbook has also been a collaboration with some individuals: Roweena Mendoza, Cathy Dreger and Hosanna Tamminga for their editing and the Dana Point Consultation Group for their invaluable input prior to the publication of the book. For all those who gave their encouragement, the authors thank you.

List of Acronyms

ACLEDA	Association of Cambodian Local Economic Development Agencies
ASA	Association for Social Advancement
ASCA	Accumulating Savings and Credit Association
AYNI	Center for Promotion of Andean Development
BRAC	Bangladesh Rural Advancement Committee
CARE	Cooperative American Relief Everywhere
CASHPOR	Credit and Savings for the Hardcore Poor
CCB	Cambodia Community Building
CDO	Christian Development Organization
CEO	Chief Executive Officer
CMED	Christian Microenterprise Development
CRWRC	Christian Reformed World Relief Committee
ED	Executive Director
FIME	Fondo de Inversiones para el Desarollo de la Microempresa
FINCA	Foundation for International Community Assistance
IGA	Income Generating Activity
KMBI	Kabalikat Para sa Maunlad na Buhay, Inc.
LEAP	Local Enterprise Assistance Program
NGO	Non-Government Organization
MED	Microenterprise Development
MEDA	Mennonite Economic Development Associates
MFI	Microfinance Institutions
MIS	Management Information Systems
OI	Opportunity International
Project L.I.F.E.	Project Love in the Family Environment
ROSCA	Rotating Savings and Credit Association
SAT	Sinapi Aba Trust
SPA	Social Preparation Activities
SEEP	Small Enterprise Education and Promotion
USAID	United States Agency for International Development
VEDCOR	Ventures and Entrepreneurship Development Center of the Orient, Inc.
YWAM	Youth with a Mission

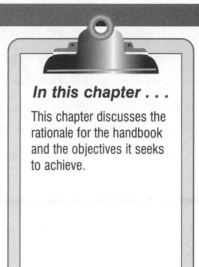

In this chapter . . .

This chapter discusses the rationale for the handbook and the objectives it seeks to achieve.

CHAPTER 1

Background

Secular microenterprise development (MED) became an increasingly popular development activity in the 1990s. Notable are the Grameen Bank, ASA, and BRAC, each reaching millions of clients. Other organizations such as ACCION and FINCA, reach tens of thousands of clients in Latin America. The success of these programs helped spawn the 1997 Microcredit Summit, which aims to mobilize credit and other financial and business services to 100 million poor people by the year 2005.

Christian development organizations (CDOs), such as OI and MEDA, have been implementing MED for over 25 years

> *The 1997 Microcredit Summit projected the provisions of credit and financial services to 100 million poor people by the year 2005*

and have since been joined by many other CDOs, including World Relief, World Vision, Food for the Hungry International, World Concern, and Enterprise Development International. While some of these organizations have substantial outreach, none of them have as yet reached the scale levels of leading secular MED programs and institutions. Many of these do seek to reach scale, but such expansion

> *MED is a development strategy that provides a broad package of financial services...as well as other business development services*

would require access to large volumes of capital that are usually available only from secular donors and equity investors. With this secular money comes secular constraints that focus primarily on the financial aspects of microfinance. As a result, it is becoming increasingly difficult for Christian MED programs to maintain the intentionality of holistic transformation while depending on secular funds for expansion.

MED is a development strategy that provides a broad package of financial services (savings, credit, and insurance) as well as other business development services (business training, marketing assistance, etc.) to entrepreneurs and the poor to enable them to operate their own productive economic activities. It seeks to serve a spectrum of people ranging from the sidewalk vendor requiring US$5 of working capital to the furniture maker with 10 employees and perhaps $50,000 in working capital. Microfinance (savings, credit, and insurance services) is one component of MED. Microfinance and MED are not the same things, and it is important to distinguish between them. This handbook asserts that

CMED is an integrated, holistic approach.

The success of both secular and Christian MED programs has spawned efforts and interest in MED among many Christian organizations, missions, and local churches. While some Christian organizations perceive MED as a way to attract donor funds that can support other activities and initiatives, many do indeed seek to promote holistic transformation among the people they serve. Missionaries, particularly in the 10-40 Window, are beginning to see MED as an entry platform to gain visas in closed countries as well as to build God's kingdom. But, as with any development fad, there are dangers that implementers (and those that support them) need to be aware of.

> The success of both secular and Christian MED programs has spawned efforts and interest in MED among many Christian organizations, missions and local churches

The incorrect application of financial services in MED programs can cause harm to borrowers and savers, as well as to families, local churches, communities, and the organizations that implement or may attempt to implement MED programs. While most secular technical donors push for rapid scaling-up, such rapid growth generates severe strain that can actually destroy an organization if it lacks the capacity to structure and manage it properly. MED implementers need to be aware of such risks.

CDOs that plan to embark on the MED journey should study its implications and potential pitfalls before commencing. Nevertheless, there remains great potential for MED to be an effective strategy in the Christian mandate of discipling the nations. MED can provide access to communities, it can address some of their physical and social needs, facilitate evangelism and discipleship, and achieve this in cost-covering ways that facilitate long-term ministry.

In recognition of these concerns, the 1997 Dana Point Consultation[2] identified a need to generate information materials, including booklets of models by CDOs and missions groups, for use by mission organizations and CDOs desiring to implement MED as an entry point for new mission initiatives. This handbook provides an overview of the basic knowledge and concepts in planning, implementing and evaluating Christian MED programs.

Objectives of the Handbook

The objective of this book is to provide information and concepts useful for designing, implementing, and evaluating Christian MED programs. It does not seek to develop every aspect of Christian MED. The book will provide information to help Christian MED practitioners and donors better understand how to apply Christian MED in ways that help proclaim Christ's kingdom. It particularly targets organizations which seek to implement a small to medium-scale program that reaches hundreds to several thousand people. The book draws on the increasingly large volume of literature available on best practices of microfinance, using eight case studies of Christian MED programs around the world to present some of the most important issues, i.e., Vision and Mission, MED Methodologies, Financial

> *The book will provide information to help Christian MED practitioners and donors better understand how to apply Christian MED in ways that help proclaim Christ's Kingdom*

Performance, Risk Management Leadership and Governance, Spiritual Transformation Strategies, and other strategic issues. Where possible, the book compares the case studies with secular MED standards to identify both weaknesses and strengths of Christian MED as well as deficiencies that need to be addressed.

CHAPTER 2

How to Develop Vision and Mission for Christian MFIs

In this chapter . . .

This chapter discusses the crucial elements of vision and mission that every Christian MED program should have. It also explores how this vision and mission should be marketed and sustained.

Christian Microenterprise Development

The ultimate concern of Christian MED is to *open the community to experience the Kingdom of God*. Christian development workers are committed to sharing Christ's blessings with the poor as disciples witnessing to His love. Through microenterprise development programs they are able to assist people to escape the lowest levels of poverty. But Christian MED involves more than economic activities. The purpose of creation is to find fulfilment in the Kingdom of God. The Church is the instrument that opens the world to its destiny in the Kingdom. Through their activities, Christian MED can strengthen the Church by restoring people to their identity and enable them to realize their role as stewards of creation and as servants of others. Effective Christian MED is spirtually focused, with strong leadership, is values-based, results sensitive and financially sound. (See Annex B)

The essential attributes of Christian MED

Vision and mission are the critical factors in Christian MED work. A driving vision is essential to motivate field workers to continue slogging through adverse conditions in slums to serve the poor. It is also a crucial element for keeping a MED program on track in both its spiritual transformation and microfinance objectives. A vision is something that must be owned and sustained by the stakeholders of the organization.

"Christian" development has five key attributes. The following checklist may serve as a guide to review the vision and mission of MED programs:

- *Does the vision support the belief in the necessity for a personal relationship with Jesus Christ?* Christian development implies that a personal relationship with Jesus Christ as Lord and Savior is necessary for a person to become what God intended him or her to be.

- *Does the vision contend that Christian development must have its foundations in a Biblical worldview?* It recognizes that unbiblical thinking and worldviews of both rich and poor cause much of the poverty and oppression in the world.

- *Does Christian development include the Church (both global and local)?* The local church is the primary institution that God has chosen to extend His king-

> *"God has chosen to extend his kingdom."*

dom. Christian MED programs that wish to build God's kingdom must serve the local church.

> *Christian development has economic, social, psychological and political elements in addition to spiritual concerns*

- *Does the mission include work for the holistic development of people?* Christian development seeks to enable people and communities to move beyond meeting their basic human needs. It has economic, social, psychological, and political elements in addition to spiritual concerns.

- *Does the mission reflect an understanding of the multi-dimensional nature of deprivation?* Christian development understands and attempts to address the complicated and integrated nature of oppression and deprivation in the lives of the poor. Deprivation is not merely economic poverty. It is multi-dimensional in its causes and effects. It is caused by sinful choices and unbiblical worldviews. Deprivation reveals itself in multiple ways that interact to deepen misery and suffering. It includes poverty, physical weakness, vulnerability, isolation, powerlessness, and broken relationships with God, self, fellowman, and creation.[3]

The Importance of Vision

Vision for Development

In today's world, vision is even more important for Christian MED programs because *secular donors and sustainability standards drive* much of the MED industry and create many of the tensions between balancing spiritual transformation with MED program sustainability.

Unfortunately, development practitioners tend to bypass vision and focus directly on policies and delivery mechanisms. This is dangerous. CDOs need to have a clear understanding of the vision God wants for the target group and communities. A phrase used by a number of Christian missionaries and CDOs is "transformation." One Christian non-government organization (NGO) defines transformation in one of its MED procedures manuals as "the change in values and perceptions which leads to a more loving pattern of action. This change can be economic, social, political or spiritual."[4] If a developmental vision such as this is the driving force behind an organization, *mission drift* from intentional spiritual transformational activities can easily result. Such a broad definition implies that persons of other faiths can be "transformed" without necessarily coming into a saving relationship with Jesus Christ. Whilst this is correct at a physical level, it falls short of God's intention for all to be reconciled to Him through Christ. Christians recognize that total transformation can occur only through a relationship with Jesus Christ. To ensure that all development work, including MED and microfinance, become explicit partners in evangelism, stimulate conversion to Christ, enable growth in discipleship, and strengthen the local church, it is essential that the five preceeding attributes of Christian MED be made explicit in organizational vision and mission statements.

> *Mission drifts from intentional spiritual transformational activities can easily result*

Vision for Sustainability

Vision for sustainability is not negotiable or optional – it is central to MED. It anticipates how a program plans to pay for its services and develops appropriate organizational structures and systems for medium and long-term survival. This is particularly important when people external to the community are involved in providing the MED services. It is also critical when considering volunteer-driven MED initiatives.

One of the major attractions of MED to both practitioners and donors is its potential to deliver beneficial services to the poor over a long period of time on a sustained basis with minimal external subsidy. MED offers the potential to move beyond the constant injection of new funds into development efforts to keep the respective ministries alive. But sustainability is not easy to achieve, even for programs that focus almost purely on financial services alone. Full financial self-sufficiency is, however, the primary concern of most secular donors. Christian MED programs that depend on secular funding must be able to meet secular financial standards or risk losing secular funding.

> *Vision for sustainability is not negotiable or optional*

For Christian MED programs with a broader holistic vision, one of the main struggles is balancing the program's sustainability and survival with providing transformative services to the poor. Chuck Waterfield, a Christian microenterprise expert who has worked with MEDA and CARE, contends that MED programs should maintain a "healthy tension, continually making fine adjustments to ensure that it remains in the narrow and difficult area avoided by those who chose to overemphasize one objective over the other."[5]

There will always be tradeoffs when a program seeks to provide excellent long term, sustainable financial services. These tradeoffs must be identified and acknowledged else there is great danger that Christian MED programs will default to only the standard of the mainstream microfinance industry—this being solely the delivery of financial services with full cost recovery.

Conflicting goals of technical donors and Christian MED organizations

As previously mentioned, the microfinance industry receives considerable funding from bi-lateral and multi-lateral technical donors. One of the major priorities of these donors is *massification* (more delicately described as scale or reach). Funding for this classification represents over 70% of all funding given to organizations that seek to increase their outreach while at the same time providing a financial return on equity. The end-goal is to convert the NGO to a for-profit institution that is structured to reach greater numbers of people. *This massification thrust of technical donors raises several issues for CMED practitioners who are motivated by God's call to minister to the poor through microfinance, i.e.,*

1. The tendency to adopt a *minimalist position (i.e., financial services only)* resulting in the reduction of support services consid-

ered necessary for meaningful transformation.

2. CMED practitioners are steered towards *accessing capital market funds* rather than grants. This deflects the local governing entity towards focusing on managing other people's money and less on impacting the community.

3. Growing internal tensions between the focus of social change and serving the poor on the one hand, and economic performance and the *criteria for a financial return* on investment on the other.

4. Maintaining *spiritual transformation activities while using western donor funds that preclude explicit evangelism and discipleship.*

5. *Inhibiting creative initiatives* in transformation with the flexibility and time required to conduct honest evaluations of value-centered issues due to the fast pace and fund-driven climate of the MED industry as well as the current emphasis on financial viability.

The challenge of massification is to avoid having to compromise the ideals of CMED. This can be partly achieved by (i) determining whether there is a Christian support base of private donors and foundations who would fund the loan portfolio and support spiritual transformation activities; and (ii) assessing the reality of accessing these resources. A balanced mix of Christian and secular donors can produce effective programs.

The Importance of local church to Christian MED

Vision for the Local Church

Discussions with MED practitioners and missionaries reveal that in many contexts there is significant distance between churches and mission organizations — and microfinance institutions (MFIs). Part of the gap is one of perception and part is reality. Some churches regard MFIs as "just businesses" with no concern for ministry. MFIs and MED programs, on the other hand, often view churches as entities that do not understand MED issues and complexities and therefore tend not to encourage on- time loan repayments. Unfortunately, there is an element of validity in both perspectives. Many MFIs shy away from the local church because few churches understand the basic tennets of microfinance, such as on-time loan repayment. Yet many Christian MFIs have given up on the local church prematurely and have not applied adequate efforts into finding ways to work with them and their members. Some MFIs are afraid to identify themselves as "Christian" fearing that it will result in repayment problems.

The Dana Point document[6] states that an effective Christian MED program "implements strategies for strengthening the local church" to be more effective in its witness. For this to happen, many Christian MED organizations and MFIs need to regain a vision for mission that sees the local church as an indispensable element of Christian development. If Christian MED

> *Some MFIs are afraid to identify themselves as "Christian" fearing that it will result in repayment problems*

organizations cannot themselves find direct ways to strengthen the local church, then they should partner with CDOs/missions, which can.

Chapter 6 discusses some specific ways by which Christian MED programs can work with local churches.

Risks in marketing Christian MED

Christian MED programs, particularly large ones, have a special challenge because they frequently must operate between the worlds of secular MED donors, Christian donors, missions, and churches. Secular donors often have minimalist goals for the programs they fund and preclude any use of their funds for "spiritual" ministries such as evangelism and discipleship.

Furthermore, donors are now sufficiently sophisticated to realize that microfinance activity alone does not necessarily result in poverty alleviation and that effective transformation is best stimulated through multifaceted complimentary integrated strategies of which MED is an important component. It is no longer valid or adequate to say that MED programs result in economic and business groups when the loans are so small that the maximum impact they have is to reduce the vulnerability of the poor.

Secular donors often have minimalist goals for the programs they fund and preclude any use of their funds for "spiritual" ministries such as evangelism and discipleship

Christian donors, on the othe hand, want their funds to have impact in spreading the gospel and in the growth of the Church. They have also become sufficiently sophisticated to discern that the stated promotional messages of organizations have a deep impact on the vision and actual implementation of Christian MED programs.

Seldom do MED organizations fully realize the significance of how they promote themselves. Several years ago, Kabalikat Para sa Maunlad Na Buhay, Inc. (KMBI)[7], made a bold statement when its board changed its mission statement to include intentional spiritual goals. It recognized that the statement may be offensive to some secular donors and lead to reduced funding. In the Philippine context, the risks for KMBI to make such an explicit declaration of its holistic development agenda are significantly lower than in other contexts, particularly Muslim or other anti-Christian contexts. In other contexts, particularly in countries closed to traditional missions and with restrictions on evangelism, Christian MED programs will undoubtedly need to be more circumspect.

The Imperatives for Promoting Christian MED

Time and Funding Commitment

Chapter 1 of this handbook stated that poorly implemented MED and microfinance programs can result in significant harm to borrowers and savers, to families, local churches, communities, to the organizations that implement MED, and to future organizations that may attempt it. This potential for harm is discussed more fully in Chapter 3: *one crucial way to minimize the risks of doing harm is by having long-term commitments (more than 2-3 years) to work in a given community*. The aspect of time commitment is important whether Christian workers or the church desire to *provide* MED services or *promote* them. Where Christian organizations desire to *provide* MED and microfinance services that go beyond small savings clubs already practiced, it must have a long-term commitment of 10 years or more. In this case, an initial presence by outsiders for some years (3-5) is probably crucial. After this period, the program should be able to provide technical support or find alternate sources to provide this on a regular basis. It is important for MED programs to be able to sustain the provision of their services as long as clients need them. If a Christian organization desires to *promote* MED services, then its time frame may be limited since it can appeal to existing indigenous savings schemes already understood by communities.

MED programs must also have *realistic funding sources* to generate adequate revenue so that MED services can be provided for as long as they are needed by the community. Once a MED program starts making loans, it must ensure that ongoing funds can be sourced to meet future demand for increased capital. This is critical because all finance programs rely on confidence. If borrowers do not have confidence that lenders will be able to provide additional loans, there is little incentive for

> *...funds must be sourced to meet future demand for increased capital*

them to repay their current loans.[8] When loans are fully funded by the savings of the program members (as is the case with self-help groups, savings clubs and cooperatives), the demand for external funding is not necessary.

Sustaining a Christian Vision

Multiple small compromising decisions can ultimately lead a MED program in the wrong direction. The risks of mission drift is high in CMED because of the pressure for sustainability. However, Christian vision can be better maintained by applying the following:

- Communicate the vision throughout the organization. It should be known and understood by every staff member.

- Take time to reflect on how well the organization is performing in the light of its vision.

- Measure impact, using key indicators to see whether the program is meeting its vision.

- Involve clients. Regularly connect management and board with clients and give clients a role in determining appropriate methods and goals of the program.

Table 1, Annex C, summarizes the issues related to vision.

Checklist of Crucial Issues for the Vision of Christian MED Programs

☐ The organization should have a *clearly articulated holistic vision* for the transformation of the community it works with. The vision must be based on a clear understanding of the local poverty situation and the intentions of God for His creation.

☐ The organization should have *strategic plans to be intentional* with holistic transformation activities, including evangelism, discipleship, and strengthening local churches formulated by the parent network or the local organization.

☐ The MED program should have a *vision for sustainability* that ensures that financial and MED services will be provided for as long as the community needs them.

☐ The organization should have a clearly articulated vision that sees *the local church* as indispensable to Christian development.

☐ The program *should promote itself* in a way that is *consistent* with its development (transformation) vision appropriate to its context.

☐ The organization should have a well thought-out plan for being in the community for the time necessary to ensure that the desired MED services are available for people when they need them. This includes *long-term commitment and funding*.

CHAPTER 3

In this chapter . . .

This chapter discusses various methodological issues in MED such as savings and informal finance, lending methodologies and the difference between promoting and providing MED services.

MED Methodologies

The Importance of Clear Targeting

Christian MED programs need to define which economic sector they want to work with and why. There is a continuum of economic activities that MED can target which range from simple income generating activities to more complex large enterprises. (See Figure 1.)

Figure 1: Continuum of Economic Activities[9]

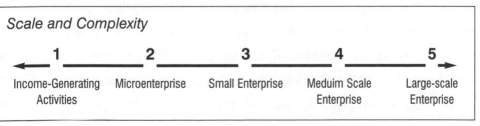

Scale and Complexity

1	2	3	4	5
Income-Generating Activities	Microenterprise	Small Enterprise	Meduim Scale Enterprise	Large-scale Enterprise

MED programs often promote that they work with the "poor" or the "poorest of the poor."[9a] But this is almost never realized in the field. For this reason, the secular Microcredit Summit has adopted a standard of the bottom 50% of people below a nation's poverty line as its target. Still, even within this target framework, the characteristics of the bottom 10% decile are very different from those of the 40-50% decile in the Summit's target.

Activity #1 of the continuum, Income-Generating Activities are typically those engaged in by clients selling merchandise on sidewalks. Of the bottom 40-50% of poor below the poverty line, these clients may be in the 15th percentile. They are very vulnerable to a broad spectrum of crises and must minimize risk of failure. These enterprises are among many survival strategies of the poor and are unlikely to grow or graduate to the next economic level. At the other end of the continuum are the large corporations with thousands of employees, and accessing large commercial loans from banks. Their investment decisions are guided by completely different criteria than sidewalk clients. In between these extremes are microenterprises (1–10 employees), small enterprises (11–50 employees), and medium-scale enterprises (51 or more employees). Evidence from MED programs around the world indicate that methodologies that work for very poor people at the Income Generating Activity level will not work for small enterprise and vice

> *At the microenterprise and small-scale enterprise level, MED can result in large income and increased employment*

versa. Impact is also different. High quality MED work at the income generation level is usually group-based and often results in the reduction of vulnerability of the clients with minimal employment opportunities. It can have relatively high impact at sustaining jobs but not at creating them. At the microenterprise and small-scale enterprise level, MED can result in increased income and employment.

Engagement at any point on this continuum impacts the poor and society. Within each point in the continuum there are "best practices" that have proven effective in serving this sector. *Proper targeting helps to ensure proper matching of the most approriate lending methodologies for the particular sector.*

Savings Programs, Instrinsic Component of MED

There is increasing evidence that the poor in most 2/3 World countries save whenever they can. Many assume that the opposite is true questioning whether the poor can save when they do not even have enough food. The fact is that people can save when money is expended (when they purchase products or services) as well as revenue– i.e., in wages, salary, profits, etc. According to expansive research on savings clubs known as Rotating Savings and Credit Associations (ROSCAs) and Accumulating Savings and Credit Associations (ASCAs) the poor worldwide have been saving in indigenous savings clubs for decades and even centuries.[10] *Many Christian implementers of MED are not aware that poor people save*, they ignore or underestimate the prevalence and power of savings. These are very significant blinders.

The poor save because they have to, but they find it extremely difficult to do so. They frequently encounter life events that are part of the fabric of communities (education, weddings, Christmas, etc.), emergencies such as illnesses or natural disasters, or opportunities that require quick cash. In addition to these are the large risks to having unsecured savings in the form of cash since their houses are usually vulnerable

Inflation significantly devalues savings

to break-in and theft. Friends or relatives in need also make frequent claims on these savings and it is often extremely difficult to deny a request for money from a relative for a sick child or an abusive alcoholic husband when there is cash hidden in the house. Inflation significantly devalues savings and clients frequently encounter the temptation of spending their savings on trivial things.

However, in spite of the difficulties of saving in the 2/3 World, evidence substantiates that the poor still persist in trying. In addition to saving money in banks (when they can), and in securities such as gold (which retains its value in inflationary times), animals and land, the poor rely on informal financial mechanisms to save.

Most governments recognize that savings are important enough to be regulated. Banks and other legal financial institutions are usually regulated by central banks, at least partly in order to protect deposits of the poor. In some contexts, MED programs are precluded from holding the savings of people for this reason. But in all cases, it is critical to understand the importance of savings, and to give the best effort applying creativity to find legal ways to help mobilize savings through safe deposit services or savings clubs.

Informal Finance

This handbook refers to *"informal finance" as "all financial transactions, loans and deposits, occurring outside the regulation of a central monetary or financial market authority."*[11] In contrast, formal finance consists of regulated financial activities, such as banks, regulated credit unions and cooperatives, legal pawnshops, insurance companies, etc. Knowledge about informal finance is not just an academic exercise. People in many countries have been members of very beneficial finance schemes that they themselves have developed and owned. Funeral funds have existed in Africa and India for many years. ROSCAs have existed in many cultures for decades or centuries (up to 600 years in Japan – well before modern banking developed in Europe).[12] As Christians we rejoice that God's common grace has extended informal financial activities to the poor in various ways.

The poor have been extremely creative in devising innovative ways to manage their money. Most informal finance is very well adapted to geographic social and economic conditions of society, and has great capacity to adjust as socio-economic and financial conditions change. Informal finance schemes have three important elements:[13]

- They take place among people who know each other.

- They involve relatively small amounts of money.

- They have multiple functions. Credit may be mixed with trade and commerce, insuring the parties against risk. Informal sav-

ings mechanisms may also provide social security and may
bring unity to communities.
Because of this, they are very
attractive to poor households.

ROSCAs and ASCAs are extremely
interesting mechanisms established by
people in many countries and deserve
brief description here.

ROSCAs

> What's in a name?
> In Kenya, ROSCAs
> are called "merry-go-
> rounds." In
> Francophone Africa
> and Cambodia they
> are called "tontines."
> In Indonesia –
> "arisans," in the
> Philippines –
> "paluwagans," and in
> India – "chits"

- *Size and Purpose*. A group of
  people, often 15 to 30 (although
  reaching on some occasions 50 or 60), join together and each
  agree to save a fixed amount of money every week (or at other
  regular intervals) to contribute to a "prize." When each meeting
  occurs and the contributions are totaled, one member of the
  group wins the entire amount or "prize." This happens until every
  member has received the prize.

- *Use of funds*. ROSCA members use their prizes for many pur-
  poses, including consumption, consumer goods, housing, education, entrepreneurial investment, etc.[14]

- *Longevity*. Once all members have benefited, the ROSCA in theory ceases, although it is often renewed and may eventually
  become a ROSCA that continually rolls over. The fact that

ROSCAs inevitably cease makes the amount of funds that they intermediate between the members time-bound. ROSCAs are symmetrical in terms of payments in and payments out and they are time-bound – they begin and end.

- *Attraction to Members*. One strength of ROSCAs is that they are extremely simple and transparent in how money is handled.

ASCAs

- *Methodology*. ASCAs are not necessarily time-bound and the members do not necessarily have to contribute the same amount every week or withdraw at any specified time.

- *Examples*. Savings & Credit Cooperatives, Credit Unions, Burial Societies, etc.

- *Longevity*. ASCAs can continue or discontinue as the members determine.

- *Functions*. Some ASCAs exist primarily to provide insurance services to their members, such as the fire insurance ASCAs formed in the slums of Bangladesh.

- *Challenges*. ASCAs may have similar transparency as ROSCAs if they are time-bound, but if savings begin to build up and are not withdrawn, accountability can be a problem. Members have a committee or a manager to run the scheme. As the fund grows, more skill is required for accountability.

- *Interest*. Non-insurance ASCAs often charge interest on loans made to members. Inflation becomes a significant factor in determining these interest rates since ASCAs try to protect the value of their members' savings. Rutherford found that ASCA interest rates in South and Southeast Asian countries with moderate inflation over the last 30 years range from 3% to 8% flat rate per month, sometimes more. In urban areas where income-generating opportunities are higher, they often charge 10% per month.

ASCAs and ROSCAs are very attractive to the poor – they are relatively simple yet have potentially high impact. They are usually well understood by the poor. It is possible to have sustainable long-term user-owned savings clubs like ROSCAs or ASCAs, but generally such clubs are linked to organizations that provide oversight which solve some of the problems of growth mentioned in the previous paragraphs. In particular, many ASCA savings clubs become virtual credit unions, they then join a formal credit union network which supervises and regulates them.[15] These networks help them manage their excess cash (not active as loans) by lending it to other credit unions requiring increased capitalization (usually younger organizations). This network can offer credit unions legal registration and protection from government authorities which seek to take

> *NGOs and missionaries considering microfinance and/or MED activities need to research which schemes exist in communities...and to what extent they are either helping the poor or further perpetuating poverty*

advantage of them.

Both ROSCAs and ASCAs are extremely important savings tools in the 2/3 World. NGOs and missionaries considering microfinance and/or MED activities need to research which schemes exist in communities, e.g. informal financial mechanisms such as ROSCAs and ASCAs, and to what extent they are either helping the poor or further perpetuating poverty. If this aspect is ignored, harm can result affecting those who belong to them. In some cases, it will be prudent to stimulate such schemes in new contexts.

A core set of lending methodologies effectively used by MED programs has been identified through experience over the past 25 years. These are briefly summarized in Table 2, Annex C.[16]

The difference between promoting MED and providing MED

As outsiders to the community, there are three basic ways to ensure that MED/microfinance services are provided to the poor. One approach is that of *MED promoters, "those who help the poor set up their own program or self-managed schemes."* The second approach is that of the *MED providers, "those who **sell** financial services to the poor."*[17] The third approach is *partnering with an existing MED provider*.

Providing MED Services occurs when an outsider, such as a MED organization, establishes and operates a microfinance program for the community. This is the primary model in the current microfinance industry since it clearly offers possibilities for dramatic cost reductions through economies of scale. In this model, borrowers are considered "clients" and the MED programs operate through more professional and business standards than the standards applied to most social development organizations. Some of the larger programs, which primarily provide microfinance services, are known as microfinance institutions (MFIs). MFIs usually seek to become banks for the poor. Most large Christian MED programs accept that there must be a balance between business-like MED disciplines and the gospel imperatives.

> *Promoting MED services helps the poor establish their own financial systems which they own and/or manage*

There are cases, particularly in India, where churches and private individuals provide financial services to communities, especially by operating ROSCAs, marriage funds, funeral funds, etc.[18] These efforts have, through experience, identified the appropriate number of members in order to attain sufficient economies of scale to make their risk manageable.

Promoting MED services helps the poor establish their own financial systems which they own and/or manage. A church or community group forms its own savings club (such as a ROSCA or ASCA) with potential for loans to members. In some cases this could be a credit union model. Involvement of external support may include training the group in basic MED methodologies and helping them develop their systems and accountability structures. The formation of this savings club could eventually lead to a linkage with an MFI.

Partnering in MED occurs when a local church or community group links with an existing MED program that will provide microfinance services to the target group. This could be a cooperative, MFI, bank, NGO, etc. It requires that the existing program be acceptable and credible to the local group or church. Where an outsider is involved, they help facilitate this linkage.

Understanding the distinction between promoting, providing and partnering in MED is important. Experience and research indicate that there are at least six important aspects that Christian workers must consider to determine whether they want to promote, provide or partner in MED services. These are:

- *Time Horizon.* To provide microfinance the organization and its people must be committed to work long-term in the given location. Continuous follow-up technical support must be provided and levels of realistic external funding for the MED program must be assured (refer to p. 15).

- *Sustainability.* MED services (as opposed to loans), including the salaries of outside workers, must be paid for and the source of grants identified.

- *Direct services.* The MED services to be provided directly to clients must be feasible with the MED approach chosen.

- *Goals for Outreach.* The number of clients to be reached must be calculated and match the approach.

- *Linkages.* Linkages with other programs should be made identifying what and from whom financial services (i.e., savings, loans, and insurance services) will be obtained.

- *Macroeconomic and Political Conditions.* Assess whether the inflation rate is so high that savings are no longer used by the poor. Ascertain whether the political and economic elite are making it impossible to manage money without unreasonable bribery and corruption.

A summary is shown in Table 3, Annex C.

Understanding the potential damage resulting from poorly conceived programs

The evidence from most 2/3 World countries is that development finance often is distorted and misused when implemented by government agencies.[19] MFIs, NGOs, and mission organizations providing financial services in a poorly conceived, designed and implemented (and ultimately unsustainable) way may actually cause more harm than good in local communities. The negative effects of bad microfinance manifests itself in various ways.

- It can cause loss of assets for clients resulting in weak businesses;

- the loan program can end up insolvent;

- effective informal credit systems can be weakened;

- credit cultures can be damaged;[20] and

- churches can be fragmented.

The following are some of the ways that MED can be incorrectly implemented:

- *Inappropriate loans* may bury an individual or a community in debt, in some cases forcing the poor to liquidate assets to pay the loans off, making them worse off post-loan than pre-loan. Some loan programs actually seize assets of their clients upon default, including their pots and pans. This may be reasonable particularly if the client has been deceitful.

- Some microfinance practitioners feel that *subsidized credit* (credit that is priced more cheaply than the cost to deliver it) damages the enterprise of those it is designed to help by not teaching them how to compete in a real market environment.

- *Low repayment rates*. Loans which are not repaid obviously reduce the confidence of finance providers in working with the target group. This will inevitably increase the costs to clients, both through higher interest rates and fees, as well as aspects such as more frequent meetings resulting in wasted productive time in order to prove credit worthiness to the lenders.

- *Local government programs*. The evidence from most 2/3 World countries is that external development finance often is frequently misappropriated and misused when implemented by government agencies.

- *Unfair preferences*. Churches can be fragmented when a MED program gives preference to believers or certain cliques of believers, particularly when church members do not fully understand the responsibilities of repaying a loan. Some may leave the church when it is unable to prevail on the organization to cancel or adjust the loan. This type of collateral damage can

> *MED programs must have clear intentionality and mechanisms to actually enforce loan repayment*

best be minimized by ensuring that all borrowers understand their obligations for on-time repayment. MED programs must then have clear intentionality and mechanisms to actually enforce loan repayment.

Special Issues: Agricultural Credit

Christian workers desiring to do credit in rural agricultural contexts must accurately estimate the debt capacity and risk structure faced by the target groups. This is not an easy exercise, as has been partly demonstrated by the failure of most agricultural credit schemes in the 2/3 World. There are three vital factors in agricultural lending which must be assessed accurately:

- *Estimate how much cash the borrower is likely to have after all costs of production of the business are subtracted*. This requires (a) estimating the production and consumption of the borrower (subsistence needs), (b) amount received for the product, and (c) the costs of all inputs used in production.

- *Estimate and quantify all "senior claims"*[21] that the borrower is likely to consider more important than the repayment of the loan. These could be food, fuel, school fees, emergency expenditures, important social obligations and ceremonies, repayment of informal lenders (including money lenders) and indigenous savings schemes (such as ROSCAs).

- *Assess the likely problems during the loan.* What are the possible implications from emergencies and other adversity on the cash flow of the enterprise? These include weather-related problems, economic uncertainty, and other risks the client is likely to face. For agricultural loans, it is vital to assess the risks of poor harvest and how frequently these are likely to occur.

Checklist of Crucial Issues on Methodology

☐ The target group must be clearly identified and its characteristics adequately communicated to serve as a guide in formulating the program design and its implementation.

☐ There must be a clear understanding of the importance of savings and demonstrated creativity in designing new savings services or in using/improving existing savings services.

☐ There should be a clear understanding of the importance of informal finance, how it can both benefit and hurt communities and how it can be used effectively to help accomplish the goals of the MED program.

☐ It must be recognized that inappropriate MED approaches can actually destroy the program making the loan, as well as the effective informal credit systems such as ROSCAs and ASCAs, credit cultures and churches in its area.

☐ The potential for self-destruction must be recognized. It must be ensured that all borrowers understand their obligations for on-time repayment, and that discipline will be seriously enforced.

☐ The underlying differences between promoting, providing, and partnering MED services must be understood. The vision and context of the organization must appear amenable to the methodolgy deployed.

☐ The program should be implemented according to sound MED methodological design principles proven to best alleviate poverty and stimulate enterprise development.

☐ There must be a clear process of making the necessary assessments in order to minimize default in agricultural loans.

CHAPTER 4

Financial Soundness of MED Programs

In this chapter . . .

This chapter discusses the crucial financial issues of Christian MED. It looks at legitimate concerns of secular MED such as the importance of knowing one's market, having a low tolerance for default and the appropriate setting of interest rates

Tensions between Christian and secular MED relating to financial soundness

Christian MED programs must have a broader vision for their MED work as opposed to their secular microfinance counterparts which focus almost exclusively on financial soundness or sustainability. In a sense, financial soundness is a *means* to an *end* for the poor receiving or participating in holistic MED that will help transform their lives. The danger of mainstream microfinance is that the means may actually *transform* the ends, in that the preoccupation with sustainability changes the decisions that alter, limit, diminish, or even eliminate the 'services' initially intended. In the worst case scenario, the original mission objective can gradually change to the point where financial sustainability is the only goal.[22]

Secular MED donors (particularly bilateral and multilateral donors) place tremendous pressure for sustainability on all MFIs, including Christian MED programs, for several reasons:

- They want microfinance programs to survive and expand to reach increasing numbers of the poor.

- They feel that local capital markets are more reliable sources of funds for expansion.

Sustainability targets are direct mechanisms to ensure that the most efficient providers of microfinance services survive and the inefficient ones are weeded out.

For as long as Christian MED programs cannot cover their costs through client-generated income or income from other investments, they will be dependent on external subsidies. As stated in Chapter 3, Christian MED programs must seek ways to ensure that the services for the poor are provided for as long as the poor need them. This is particularly true for MED *providers*. But MED promoters face issues related to financial soundness and sustainability. This chapter also examines the crucial financial issues of Christian MED programs. It draws significantly on the criteria set at the Dana Point Consultation for effective Christian MED organizations.

Understanding the market for MED services

The first principle underlying financial soundness is the basic discipline to understand the market. "Market" here refers to both the supply side (other providers of MED and microfinance) and the demand side (what the "customer" wants or needs). MED programs must obtain adequate knowledge on the supply-side. Designing effective MED programs requires knowledge of variables such as inflation, political stability, regulatory framework,[23] and information about other providers of MED services. Research on the demand side is also necessary to identify constraints and opportunities at the client level. A good knowledge of market conditions will result in longer lasting and more effective services.

Basic MED market research in any given location should provide answers to the following questions:

- How do people manage their savings deposits? Banks and informal schemes?

- How do people temporarily convert the assets they hold (land, jewelry, etc.) into cash? Are there pawnbrokers that operate in the community?

- How do people obtain immediate access to lump sums of money now, in exchange for future savings? These are usually loans that come through MFIs, NGOs, ROSCAs, ASCAs, money lenders, cooperatives, banks, etc.

- How do people provide for known life-cycle expenses such as births, deaths, marriages, etc.?

- Where do people obtain funds to cope with emergencies?

- How do people find access to finance for small economic activities?[24]

Answering these questions provides MED implementers with in-depth knowledge of community economics, poverty, and social relations, as well as some elements of local politics. It provides essential information about other providers and promoters of microfinance services and informal finance so that Christians intending to commence MED programs can identify gaps and determine how best to fill them while minimizing damage. However, it is also possible that gaps do not exist and that they are only perceived or assumed by researchers who failed to apply in-depth analysis of the community dynamics and conditions.

Measuring financial performance

Most MED organizations seek to use the tools of finance – usually savings and loans – to stimulate poverty alleviation and/or enterprise development. These financial tools are amenable to measurement; therefore MED programs themselves should be designed to be able to accurately monitor their own financial performance with little difficulty. Christian MED programs must measure their performance as they steward the resources God has provided.

In practice, MED practitioners must determine which financial indicators can be utilized most efficiently and powerfully within the context of their organization. Secular microfinance consultants have devised entire manuals of financial ratios that can be used to guide their performance.[25] These are usually implemented by organizations embracing the disciplines of "best practices." These MED programs have large MIS budgets.

Smaller organizations must choose other appropriate performance indicators.

This handbook focuses on three basic domains of financial performance because they apply equally to all programs irrespective of their size:

- *Portfolio quality*, measured by "portfolio at risk;"

- *Sustainability ratios*, measured by operational and financial self-sufficiency ratios;

- *Efficiency indicators*, measured by portfolio per loan officer, number of clients per loan officer, and transaction and delivery costs.[26]

More detailed business-like ratios such as return on assets, equity ratios, etc. are difficult to use in smaller MED programs.

The microfinance industry's preoccupation with sustainability has led to the development of a number of indicators to measure how well microfinance programs are able to minimize their costs. A distinction is made between the financial performance of the loan portfolio and the efficiency of transaction and delivery costs.

Good financial indicators can be extremely useful in sifting out inefficien-

> *Good financial indicators can be extremely useful in sifting out inefficiencies. But they must always be interpreted and filtered through the stated vision, values and objectives of the program*

cies. But they must always be interpreted and filtered through the stated vision, values and objectives of the program. Frequently, programs with transformational objectives will not have client/loan officer ratios as high as MFIs applying minimalist principles. It is particularly useful for Christian MED programs to segregate the cost structure for the various services they provide in order that they can accurately measure the efficiencies of their different service areas. It is recommended to measure costs related to financial services as well as costs related to health, Bible studies, discipleship, etc. so that efficiency improvements can be clearly identified and quantified.

Accuracy is crucial. Incorrect data, particularly that of portfolio quality, will endanger an organization, which might one day wake up to discover that it has no capital to lend.

The importance of default intolerance

As we saw in Chapter 3, late loan repayment and default often generate tensions that pressure MED organizations, the community and other related organizations. Default is the main reason for excessive expenses that directly reduce the capitalization of the MED organization. *Uncontrolled and rampant default must be ruthlessly arrested because it will spread like a virus if clients detect a tolerance for it in the program.* Most secular donors require that microfinance programs acknowledge their default rate by writing-off bad loans after a certain period of time, often one year.

Arrears, or late loan payments, are equally dangerous and cause rapid downward spirals. High arrears raise the costs of providing services since staff must spend more time following up with clients. Late loan repayment can stimulate a liquidity crunch, making it difficult for loan officers to grant timely repeat loans, and decreasing client confidence in the program. Staff energy and motivation is sapped. Income is reduced since new loan revenue is reduced and staff have less time to bring in new clients.

Measuring loan repayment performance

Late loan payments can be measured in many ways. This complicates standardized methods to assess and compare programs. The microfinance industry has settled on one basic indicator: portfolio at risk. Portfolio at risk is a banking concept based on the assumption that a loan with late payments is at higher risk of default. The portfolio at risk rate is usually aged in the following categories:

- 30 days late
- 60 days late
- 90 or more days late

Portfolio at risk is calculated by the value of current loans outstanding in which payments are late over a given time period divided by the total value of all loans outstanding.[27]

MED programs that are serious about loan repayment (and their own survival) must have timely information on arrears and defaults, and must be able to report the amount of bad debt write-off and the state of the portfolio at risk. Other indicators of repayment health are useful for internal use.

An adequate capital base is critical

Financial programs are effective only when risk and confidence are balanced so that value is created for both capital suppliers and clients through financial transactions.[28] In the 2/3 World where enforcement of contract law is weak, borrowers' confidence in a loan program is based on their assuredness that the organization is stable and solvent and will be able to provide repeat loans if clients need them. If clients detect that they may not be able to obtain a follow-up loan, their confidence in the MED program is weakened, reducing the motivation to repay their current loan. Thus, when MED programs begin to lend they must be certain that they can meet a long-term demand for their financial services. They

> *Credit users will demand access to larger loans*

must project as accurately as possible a likely loan size trajectory for their clients so that they do not expand faster than their loan capital base will allow. They must also maintain their capital base against pressures caused by default and particularly inflation, since inflation can dramatically erode the real value of a MED program's capital base.

MED programs are also frequently hit by natural and man made disasters. The healthier the loan program, the better will be its ability to survive such disasters by staying adequately liquid.[29]

Subsidies and the effects

The term subsidy is anathema to the devoted evangelists of pure microfinance and is not found in their vocabulary. Some Christian MED programs also suffer from the same delusion. Successful MED programs have a love/hate relationship with the concept of subsidization. It is caressed when it helps programs start or open up work in new areas. And it is resented because extended subsidies can hide inefficiencies. Minimalist programs are disadvantaged when they operate in areas with other programs that are heavily subsidized because they create "unfair competition."

CDOs desiring to implement MED must understand the following points about subsidization

- *Subsidy is not intrinsically evil or anti-developmental.* In fact, even though some microfinance people do not like to admit it, subsidy is inherent in almost all models of finance. Banking systems in many countries are based on a foundational subsidy of government-backed deposit insurance and government oversight and regulation. Financial systems are also founded on institutions such as legal systems that allow the enforcement of contracts, retain public order, etc. – many of which are subsidized through the taxpayers of that nation.

> *Subsidies are frequently used to disguise inefficiencies*

- *In microfinance and MED, it is well established that not every client pays the full costs of services provided.* In particular, clients that are new to a program and/or those with smaller loans tend to be subsidized by clients with more experience in the program and/or bigger loans.

- *In most cases, subsidy is inevitable at the time of start-up.* Almost all microfinance programs, even those that now officially oppose subsidy, at one time inevitably had large external subsidies to get them started.

- *Sustained local subsidy is less dangerous than external subsidy.* One such example is the VED-COR program where a local Philippine church with a holistic vision established a training arm to help train other local churches to do holistic Christian MED. The salary, office space, etc. are provided by the local church, not paid for with interest earned from cooperative members. This is a different type of subsidy than if foreign donors had funded VEDCOR. In this instance, there is a greater degree of local national ownership and accountability.

> *External or internal subsidy should never be used to hide or mask inefficiency at any level*

- Because subsidy is not inherently evil, it is up to each respective MED organization to decide when subsidy may be justifiable in its continuing operations, particularly for MED promoters who fully realize the benefits and limitations of their work.

- *External or internal subsidy* (when clients subsidize each other) *should never be used to hide or mask inefficiency at any level.* MED practitioners have unequivocal accountability to our Lord and the community.

> Subsidized MED programs which fail can damage the credit culture simply by not surviving – this breaks down the trust of the community for other MED organizations

- *External subsidy should not be used to reduce the interest rate charged to borrowers to below the actual costs of providing the financial services.*[30] Interest rates are the most important component in a loan program's survivability. It is potentially less damaging to apply subsidy to start-up costs, costs of expansion into new areas, costs of piloting new experiments, or other transformation services than to apply them to the operational viability of the program.

- Poorly implemented MED which is often highly subsidized, can damage communities and other MFIs (see Chapter 3 discussion). Among some MED providers, there exist high levels of external subsidy. This masking of inefficiency is unfair competition that can harm other microfinance programs which are serious about sustainability and serving the poor long term. Subsidized loans could undercut these programs by having unrealistically low interest rates which draw clients away from the non-subsidized programs, or drive down the interest rates of other MED programs delaying their sustainability. *Subsidized MED programs which fail can damage the credit culture* simply by not surviving – this breaks down the trust of the community for other MED organizations.

- Hidden indirect subsidization. This occurs in group loan schemes where clients cross guarantee each other. The default rate is concealed as superficially it appears that all members repaid their respective loans. In effect some clients are subsidizing other delinquent members who may have legitimate reasons or just inefficient enterprises.

Christian MED programs should clearly identify subsidy goals for each program component. A strong conclusion of this research is that in order to avoid doing harm and to maximize long-term impact, all finance-related elements of a MED program should eventually be funded by interest and fees from the users of the financial services. These program components often include:

- Individual training
- Group capacity building
- Loan capital
- Operating expenses
- Insurance expenses
- Other finance activities (such as ROSCAs, co-ops, health insurance, funeral funds, etc.

Implications of self-reliance

The intention of secular donors is that revenue from interest, fees and investments completely covers all program costs within a determined period of (generally) 3-7 years. This occurs gradually as programs move from subsidy-dependence towards operational self-sufficiency where all operational costs of the program (including salaries, travel, other administrative expenses, interest paid on borrowed funds, and loan loss provision) are covered.[31] Eventually MED programs are to attain financial self-sufficiency where inflation is factored in as a cost and grants are given an imputed cost.[32] To achieve financial self-sufficiency, many programs become minimalist and focus solely on the provision of financial services.

During the gestation and design stage of any Christian MED program, implementers must decide how they will fund the program's various components. Particular attention must be given as to what will be subsidized and for how long. Obviously this is directly related to the vision and mission of the organization, whether it seeks to promote or provide MED services. A realistic estimate of the program's ability to maintain subsidy long enough to facilitate sustainable impact is imperative.

MED implementers and donors need to realize that there will be little surplus, if any, from the revenue of the loan program to fund diverse programs and services without overburdening borrowers with interest for services they may not want. Llanto's (1999) research on selected case studies in the Philippines found that in order to perform minimal spiritual transformation activities upwards of 15% are added to the operational costs of the program.[33] Christian MED programs need to find alternate sources of funds for these expenses.

The effects of borrowing commercially

A stated goal of "best practices" MFIs is to transition from dependence on donor grants to eventually relying on market capital funds to cover portfolio growth, with other funds for expansion coming from operating profits. The assumption is that positioning microfinance growth work clearly on international and local capital will result in the most efficient delivery of financial services.[34] This may in fact be true. But relying solely on borrowed funds entails major implications. One is that higher-cost MED programs may eventually be forced to close or merge with more efficient microfinance operations. While this may be acceptable as an economic philosophy, it raises the question as to what happens when the MED world is reduced to purely minimalist microfinance providers. Will there be room left for Christian MED programs that have broader holistic goals based on Biblical understandings of poverty and development? Will Christian MED programs be forced to water down their vision and objectives in

> *Borrowing commercially may compromise the vision*

order to survive in a highly competitive minimalist microfinance arena?

Christian MED programs need to be extremely cautious about borrowing commercial funds, particularly if those funds come with strings attached that will compromise the vision and objectives.

One issue faced by Christian MED programs today is dealing with some donors who now want to be seen as investors with representatives on the organization's board of directors. Christian MED organizations must have the courage to maintain their holistic agenda in these situations. Of course, there are contextual issues that can mitigate against compliance, but every attempt to retain integrity must prevail.[35]

Issues in setting an appropriate interest rate

The topic of interest rates can be controversial among evangelical Christians. Some proponents interpret Old Testament passages of precluding charging interest to other Israelites as directly applicable for not charging interest in the 21st century. This position does not appreciate the current context of capitalist cash-based economies, which are totally different from the land-based agrarian economy of the Old Testament. *The authors of this handbook believe that evangelical Christians can charge interest without violating scriptural guidelines.*[36]

The issue of interest in Christian MED can be extremely divisive, particularly for providers of MED/microfinance services who must set interest rates. MED promoters can let the savings groups determine the rate of interest they want to charge each other. The researchers of this study were surprised at the extremely high interest rates charged in ASCAs.

Research reveals a direct correlation between financial soundness and membership in a MED support network

Theoretically, interest is simply the price of capital; this is no different than the expenses of equipment, land, or working capital in a business. Charging rent for a house, car, or office space is theoretically the same as charging interest to borrow capital. However, the poor's need for access to credit is periodically so intense (due to family emergencies or life-cycle needs), cash-rich capital suppliers (known as loan sharks, cayotes, etc.) can take advantage of their vulnerability by charging usurious rates of interest.

Interest charged on credit extended is required to pay for the following expenses related to transaction, delivery and recovery costs:

- Provision of services, including employees, office, travel, supplies, equipment (including depreciation), etc.

- Losses from clients who default on loans.

- Raising capital for the loan portfolio.

- Interest payments where a program holds people's savings.

- Cost of borrowing money.

- For self-owned finance groups, such as ASCAs, interest charges may fund dividends or profits for its members.

The current evidence from mainstream programs is that *interest rates are the most powerful determinant as to whether an MFI can cover its costs.*[37] Setting an appropriate interest rate requires answering the following questions:

1. *What is the prevailing inflation rate?* Inflation erodes the value of the capital base. Interest rates and fees are the best concrete tool to maintain capital value without going to external sources for recapitaliza-

tion. It is especially important to maintain the value of a loan portfolio where clients' savings are compensating for inflation.

2. *To what extent are clients demanding financial services?* This is measured partly by observing how clients are using local informal services and what interest rates they are paying, as well as

> *Interest is simply the cost of borrowing*

measuring how the community is using formal services such as banks, pawnshops, other credit programs, etc. This information determines what the market will bear.

3. *What are the operating and financial costs?* It is crucial to keep operating costs to a minimum especially if it is necessary to borrow capital to finance loan activities.

4. *What are the arrears and default rates?* Defaults and arrears need to be controlled tightly since they affect both cost and income. Interest rates must reflect the realistic levels of default.

Check List of Crucial Financial Issues

☐ Financial sustainability must be viewed as a means and not an end.

☐ The market environment must be adequately understood in terms of the end users' financial service needs, as well as the macro-economic and political conditions that impact its services.

☐ Default intolerance must be clearly reflected in the organization's objectives, as should low arrears and low portfolio at risk. The imperative for adequate systems to monitor arrears is an essential management task.

☐ There must be clearly defined and operationalized sustainability objectives. There must be a nuanced understanding of how and what the program plans to subsidize, particularly its holistic development and transformation objectives.

☐ There must be a prudent strategy for leveraging and borrowing funds, insolvency indicators must be designed and monitored closely remaining intentional in their transformation agenda and at the same time minimizing risk.

☐ Efficiency targets must be established that allow room for intentional spiritual transformation activities. The program must measure up to its targets.

☐ Interest rates must be structured and computed accurately to cover the costs of financial services in order for those services to become eventually sustainable.

CHAPTER 5

Leadership and Governance in Christian MED

In this chapter . . .

This chapter discusses aspects of leadership and governance in Christian MED programs i.e. types of leaders, local leadership, continuity and adaptability

The importance of Leadership and Governance

High quality leadership and governance are crucial elements for success in large "best practices" MFIs as well as in small MED organizations or even ROSCAs promoted by churches or missionaries. *Effective governance keeps leadership accountable, values-focused and protects its assets* from loss due to incompetence, negligence or malpractice/corruption.

MED programs begin in different ways and take different trajectories. In many cases, a visionary person starts a program and gathers staff around him/her. As the program grows, a board is recruited and may or may not be given significant oversight authority. Other MED efforts, most often spearheaded by the ED rather than the board, are created with a clear plan for development into sustainability-focused MFIs.

While program implementation is led by strong, capable senior management, *control and accountability occur in the best secular MED programs through strong governance.* In larger scale MED, governance is defined as *"the process through which a board of directors guides an institution in fulfilling its corporate mission and protects the institution's assets."*[38]

Governance forces checks and balances between the various owners and stakeholders in MED programs. Its composition may vary over time as the market environment changes.

Governance forces checks and balances between the various owners and stakeholders in MED programs

Ownership of MED work is tightly linked to effective governance. In instances of NGO and mission-implemented MED, there is often no official ownership. Many programs operate with external NGO/mission ownership rather than for-profit corporate ownership structures.[39]

Boards of NGOs and missions are responsible to the various stakeholders in the organization (including clients, employees, donors, and providers of technical assistance, etc.) yet these board members themselves frequently have no personal investment and liability, compared to board members of profit corporations. NGO board members primarily act out of a sense of personal and social responsibility or Christian calling.

Ensuring Christian Leadership in MED

Ensuring continued Christian leadership in a MFI requires the following:

- Placing mature *Christian leaders* at the Board and *management* levels.

- Upholding a *Christian vision and mission*.

- Hiring *Christian loan officers and personnel* to interact with the local church.

Christians must lead Christian MED programs. The demands of "best practice" MED are signficant, particularly the pressure to attain self-sufficiency. These can render sustainability into an end in itself, and draw the mission away from the intended target group towards communities which can absorb increasing volumes of capital, enabling the program to reach rapid self-sufficiency.

It is for this reason that mature Christian leadership is crucial. Only Christian leadership can keep a Christian vision alive and vibrant. Where the staff has personal transformation ministries with clients (which includes evangelism and discipleship) all the personnel must be Christian.

The demands of vision-driven governance

As stated above, good governance is necessary for programs of all sizes. In one way or another, MED programs must be held accountable to higher authorities. In modern corporations, this accountability occurs primarily through a board of directors. Secular MED programs are now applying corporate governance models and have identified the following set of functions that the governing body[40] must accomplish:[41]

1. Ensure that the program meets its *legal obligations* and is protected from legal harassment or unnecessary litigation.

2. *Strategic Direction*
   - Ensure that the mission statement is clearly defined, respected, and regularly revisited.
   - Ensure effective planning by overseeing the processes of strategic, business, and action planning.
   - Provide legitimacy to the program, and shape and enhance its image.

3. *Fiduciary oversight*
   - Steward the resources of the organization, protect program property, and ensure that assets are used in ways consistent with the program's values and goals.
   - Ensure that the program has the resources necessary to implement its plans.
   - Balance short-term goals with the long-term viability of the program.

4. *Oversight of program* (not management of the program):
   - Govern the program by providing direction to management, and give management the operational authority to implement.
   - Appoint the CEO and oversee his/her performance.
   - Monitor operations and performance through board meetings, visits, reports, and internal and external audits.

- Evaluate performance relative to other MED programs.
- Assess and respond to risks, both internal and external.
- Protect the programs in times of crisis. Intervene when necessary in times of organizational distress.

5. Self-Assessment and renewal
   - Monitor and assess its own performance.
   - Maintain an active committed board.

> *Governance in MED organizations is an overview structure where vision is articulated, policies are set, and close monitoring is implemented*

Governance in MED organizations is an overview structure where the vision is articulated, policies are set, and close monitoring is implemented. It is separate and distinct from the management of an organization requiring a macro-view of the organization's directions.

To avoid the conflicts that often arise between strong professional management and a board that inadvertently micro-manages, John Carver[42] proposes the formulation of policies which embody the values and priorities of the board, operates as guidelines and parameters for management and provide a framework for decision-making both for the board and management. Policy categories are recommended by Carver to facilitate the process. These categories are:

- Impact to be achieved which covers policies on the results the organization aims to achieve;
- Operational parameters which define what is imprudent and

unethical;

- Board executive relationship which reduces the grey area between board and management functions and provides criteria for Management evaluation; and
- Governance process which defines the board's job description.

Set policies also make it simpler for boards to monitor the various areas of management operations that they have identified as needing closer scrutiny.

While all the aforementioned are vital, one of the most important tasks of governance for Christian MED programs is to protect the organizations vision by balancing the objectives of providing holistic kingdom building MED with sustainability concerns that enable the organization to achieve its transformation agendas. It is helpful to note that credit unions develop governing authorities with most of these same functions. These governing authorities are made up of the members. In the long run, MED programs that provide financial services are advised to strengthen existing governing structures to oversee management and enhance their own accountability roles. For missionaries operating in decentralized organizations, or who have supervisors with little MED experience, it may be most practical to develop a local management structure similar to a credit union where the users are also the owners.

Types of leaders required for Christian MED

Studies of secular MED programs have shown that leadership must be competent in the following functions:[43]

- Very high *devotion to the program*, involving heavy time commitments and strong identification with the future of the organization;
- Ability to maintain the vision and mission of the organization and keep it on compass;
- Sufficient *knowledge of the details of the organization* to enable the leader to know what is happening with key indicators and targets;
- Ability to *work within the local* socio-economic and political *context*
- High *ability to motivate staff* or workers through vision, and by attending to the personal and professional needs of staff;
- Ability to project and *inculcate the corporate culture* throughout the organization.

Local leadership is important for Christian MED

Christian MED programs which plan to provide long-term MED services over the long term have no choice but to be implemented, managed and governed by nationals for the following reasons:

- Trained nationals will generally be able to *better adapt MED methodologies to local contexts*.
- Trained nationals are generally not under the same pressures of

family and *governmental immigration policies* that can remove expatriates from the host country.

- Nationals can generally *deal with government officials more effectively*, and are often more effective in raising local resources.
- *Clients* tend to view nationals as less wealthy than expatriates and do not see them through the eyes of foreign donors.
- Nationals can provide services more efficiently than expatriates can.
- Where expatriates are employed to manage MED programs on

> *Where expatriates are employed to manage MED programs on expat salaries, it can be assumed that the operational costs are heavily subsidized*

expat salaries, it can be assumed that the operational costs are heavily subsidized.

The importance of continuity and adaptability in Christian MED

MED promotion programs are subject to the same pressures at the level where MED services are provided. For example, ROSCAs and savings cooperatives should be implemented and managed by nationals as should large-scale MFIs. But the promoters themselves do not necessarily have to be national workers as long as they are effective.

All personnel providing or promoting MED programs must be well trained in the corporate culture and operating procedures of the program.

This corporate culture must include the vision of the organization.

Secular MED programs that focus on microfinance alone do not generally provide skills training in project appraisal, monitoring, enterprise expansion, marketing, product development, quality of leadership improvements, and client relations because these activities are too costly.

Strong MED programs usually have a continuity of leadership which enables them to maintain their vision, mission, and trajectory. The biggest and most successful secular MED programs are still headed by their founders to this day. However, when senior management do falter, a strong board can hold a MED program together and reform it.

The leaders and governors of effective MED programs should be able to learn and adapt to changes in the context and stages of organizational growth and maturity. *Because most MED is implemented in fairly volatile socio-economic and political contexts, leaders must be vigilant about monitoring the local socio-economic and political situation as well as the performance of their programs.* It is also critical to track trends in the MED industry, and leaders should have adequate knowledge of this in order to build on proven models with each new program adaptation. This knowledge base is becoming increasingly accessible because of support organizations, such as the Small Enterprise Education and Promotion (SEEP) Network, and the numerous publications that are now emerging in the indus-

> *The leaders and governors of effective MED programs should be able to learn and adapt to changes in the context and stages of organizational growth and maturity*

try, and the internet.

Leadership and governance must also evolve to supply the needed skills required at different stages of organizational maturity. A charismatic, visionary leader who is most effective at start-up is not necessarily the best for the organization as it grows towards maturity. Most MED organizations outgrow their initial leadership, therefore it is vital that governing authorities recognize the different phases of organizational growth and make the necessary management adjustments. Such decisive action requires a high degree of credibility and trust between the leaders and the management team.

> *Most MED organizations outgrow their initial leadership*

Check List of Leadership and Governance Issues

☐ The organization must have *mature Christian leaders* with a solid and consistent vision for holistic transformation, as well as having a plan for the conversion of non-believing personnel (see Chapter 6). There must also be plans to implement spiritual ministries (See Chapter 2).

☐ There must be *competent persons* governing the program. They must attend to the following areas of governance:
  • Legal obligations
  • Strategic direction
  • Fiduciary responsibilities
  • Oversight/supervision/verification
  • Self-assessment and renewal

☐ The Board of Directors must *balance the social and sustainability agendas* of the program.

☐ There must be *leadership that is indigenous*, trained, and competent at:
  • Maintaining the vision and mission of the organization and keeping it on compass;
  • Assessing the realities of key indicators and targets, having sufficient knowledge about the organization;
  • Working within the local socio-economic and political context;
  • Motivating personnel through vision and by attending to their personal and professional needs; and
  • Projecting and inculcating the corporate culture of the organization.

- [ ] There must be *continuity of leadership*. The leadership itself must grow and mature in its understanding of the organization growth complexities. This should be reflected through a balance of continuity with the organizational requirements for professional management skills.

- [ ] There must be a *sound knowledge of Christian MED disciplines*, with the ability to change and adapt to the local context.

- [ ] There must be adequate knowledge of the current MED industry trends by the organization's leadership.

CHAPTER 6

In this chapter . . .

This chapter discusses some ways to translate the vision of spiritual transformation into intentional efforts to yield spiritual fruit in Christian MED. While there is no fixed blueprint, the experiences of other organizations and their reliance on the Holy Spirit prove fruitful.

Spiritual Transformation Strategies

The main characteristics of an effective Christian MED organization

Achieving spiritual transformation within a "best practice" microfinance framework is challenging. It requires vision, tenacity, patience, faithfulness, and commitment. The Dana Point Consultation identified three important characteristics in the category of an effective Christian MED organization:

- Led by the Holy Spirit
- Implements strategies for spiritual transformation
- Implements strategies for strengthening the local church

Chapter 2 of this handbook discussed the vision dimensions of Christian MED programs. The vision for a client's spiritual transformation includes spiritual regeneration through new birth in Jesus Christ and sanctification through the ongoing work of the Holy Spirit in the believer's life. This sanctification includes repairing broken relationships with ourselves, other people, and God's creation, as well as renewing the mind with a Biblical worldview so that thought begins to reflect the nature of God and of man, and God's redemptive purpose.

Personnel required for Christian MED organizations

While God allows poverty to exist, it was not part of God's original intention for His creation. Poverty, when understood from a Biblical perspective, is much more a characteristic of the enemy's stronghold than it is of God's kingdom. Fighting poverty necessarily becomes a spiritual battle. Christian MED programs must therefore nurture and encourage the spiritual development of their workers if they expect to have a meaningful spiritual impact on their clients.

It is important to train personnel in holistic vision, enabling them to integrate spiritual ministries into their daily work routines

CMED organizations must seek to transform themselves before they can transform their clients. Therefore, it is important to train personnel in holistic vision, enabling them to integrate spiritual ministries into their daily work routines.

The Bible commands us to pray without ceasing. Christian MED programs should bathe their work in prayer and institutionalize prayer in their organizations. Staff often find it extremely valuable to have management pray for them and conduct regular devotions so they can grow in their own faith.

When a Christian MED program hires non-believing staff for work with clients, it cannot expect them to witness to the good news that motivates Christian MED work. Thus, for such an organization to expect impact beyond the financial, it must have a deliberate plan and take action to see that its non-believing staff has every opportunity to hear the gospel and respond.

> *The organization must have a deliberate plan and take action to see that its non-believing staff has every opportunity to hear the gospel and respond*

Chapter 2 described the vision of holistic Biblical development which Christian MED programs should consider. Christian MED organizations have tried numerous models for holistic impact of their clients beyond the mere provision of financial services. They should either do evangelism and discipleship themselves or link with external partners to help them. Christian MED programs that do not have the expertise to develop certain discipleship elements, such as Biblical worldview training, should still encourage their Christian staff to share the gospel and proclaim God's kingdom. Furthermore they should link with other organizations to provide the necessary supplementary spiritual training for their personnel.

Verbal proclaimation strategies that organizations can use

Many Christian MED programs undertake evangelism and discipleship directly. In this approach, personnel use combinations of lifestyle evangelism, evangelism to individuals and groups, Bible studies, and other approaches to minister directly to people. These are generally appropriate in Roman Catholic or nominal Christian contexts. Another strategy is for Christian field workers to identify relatively strong Christians in client groups, and then mentor/disciple them so that they can do much of the ministry. This is especially useful where the MED program wants each field worker to reach a relatively high number of clients. A third strategy is to hire staff whose only task would be to facilitate spiritual transformation activities in creative ways. Field staff of programs that use individual lending may have more time to target individual clients. Group lending programs can encourage field staff to work with believers within the groups to encourage them, or the groups themselves, to be more active in proclaiming the word.

Providing valuable MED services in honest ways that regard clients with respect can be powerful pre-evangelism that helps bring people to Christ

Some Christian MED programs operate in Muslim, Hindu, Buddhist or totalitarian political contexts that are hostile to Christianity. This is often the case in the 10-40 Window. In such circumstances, Christian MED programs must be discreet. Providing valuable MED services in honest ways that regard clients with respect can be powerful pre-evangelism that helps bring people to Christ. Staff in these programs can take several approaches.

- Be available to answer questions from clients about why the program is not corrupt.[44]

- Live in ways that identify them as being Christian – such as celebrating Chirsitan events, e.g. a Christian wedding, Easter, regular church attendance.

- Identify local house churches and encourage relationships between   Christians of the house church and non-believers in the client group.

- Build relationships, mentor, and disciple church members to assist in evangelism and discipleship.

The finance methodology chosen is one determinant of the spiritual impact on clients. Evidence from one case study revealed that group-based methodologies could have higher impact in social and spiritual areas than individual-based loan programs. This was within a context of a Christian MED program that is highly concerned with its efficiency as it grows towards sustainability. This may not be true for missionaries who seek to work with individual clients and have deep impact with them.

Partnering/Networking with other NGOs

Alliances are another obvious strategy that Christian MED programs can consider in order to facilitate spiritual transformation. Retaining a focus on financial disciplines in MED is not negotiable and it is consistent with

holistic vision to link with other organizations or a local church to complement
financial services with evangelism, discipleship, and Biblical worldview training.
For MED programs that seek to grow to
scale, this is suggested as the best option.
While it requires considerable resources
and effort to train organizations in the
basics of MED (so that they understand it
well enough not to send contradictory sig-

> *Link with other
> organizations or a
> local church to
> compliment financial
> services with
> evangelism,
> discipleship, and
> Biblical worldview
> training*

nals to clients), it is well worth the effort. But choosing a partner organization must be done with care.[45]

Working in partnership requires that all organizations, including the
MED organization, set aside their natural competitive tendencies and
work together to build God's kingdom. This is not easy for many CDOs
(and even more challenging for CMED organizations), which are increasingly being pushed into competitive situations by the industry's secular
donors.

The relationship of Christian MED organizations with the local Church

*Christian MED must seek to strengthen the
local church.* Unfortunately, many Christian
MED organizations have had adverse experiences with churches, particularly when church
members fail to repay their loans on time or
when church leaders do not encourage mem-
bers to consider their loan obligations as a matter of Christian stewardship.

MED that is poorly conceived or implemented can damage the local church and church planting efforts. MED practitioners should consider the following principles to avoid this:

- *Know the contexts well.* Conduct preliminary research in the following areas before starting MED efforts:

> *MED that is poorly conceived or implemented can damage the local church and church planting efforts*

- Religious context

- Socio-political context

- Economic context

- *Plan preparatory training* and regular workshops of stewardship and accountability principles and biblical values of wealth creation.

- Regularly remind church members and leaders that it is virtuous to repay loans and that repaying loans will strengthen the church.

> *Capital that derives from people's savings is more likely to be better stewarded than funds from external donors*

- *Do not involve pastors in decision-making on dispensing loans or loan collection.* These may be compromised by what church members might perceive as contradictions (grace and forgiveness versus repayment discipline).

- *Mobilize savings for MED capital build-up*. This can help church members move beyond their perception that Christian development consists of "dole-outs" rather than self-help. This approach may be slower, but capital which is derived from savings is more likely to be better stewarded than funds from external donors.[46]

- *Recognize that the poor will face emergencies*. Be prepared by establishing or facilitating savings and insurance schemes that can help clients in such situations.

- *Encourage the church to develop other diaconal support services*/mercy ministries to complement the MED program and help people in need.

- *When outside money is involved, structure the MED program so that it has a "para-church" identity in the local community*. This can be especially helpful when communities expect churches to engage in other dole-out activities with limited accountability.

- Partner *with organizations that can provide discipleship services or worldview training*.

Strategies where there is an existing local Church

From the perspective of local churches, missionaries, and national pastors, there are several ways for local churches to use MED as a tool for holistic ministry. One is to partner with an existing MFI (either Christian or non-Christian), savings and credit cooperative, or MED program; then MED services can be accessed from that organization, particularly where the program has credibility with the local church and its leadership. In this scenario, local churches can access microfinance products and benefit from them by limiting the membership of their group to believers. Or, they can use the MED program as a tool for building relationships that result in evangelism, discipleship, and church planting.

> *Use the MED program as a tool for building relationships that result in evangelism, discipleship and church planting*

Another possibility for churches to engage in MED is to establish their own program. Considering the principles listed above, it is recommended that churches utilize the strengths of savings capital and implement systems that local people already understand – such as ROSCAs or ASCAs – rather than access outside capital. After several years of success in managing a ROSCA or ASCA, a local church can approach an MFI institution and access their financial services.

Strategies where there is no existing local church

MED is at the frontier as a strategy of mission for unreached areas in the 10-40 Window. Three cases in the research for this handbook operated in dominant Muslim or Buddhist context. Two cases found that operating as MED organizations of excellence and integrity, their word was an important way to demonstrate Christian behavior and the love of Christ to non-believers. These are important pre-evangelistic strategies. One case in Thailand focused on helping believers – another essential strategy for countries in the 10-40 Window where people are marginalized and ostracized for converting to Christianity.

Individual missionaries, who are not seeking to establish an MFI operating with "best practices" industry standards, must realize that MED is a complex development strategy and should not be regarded simply as a tool to obtain a visa. Such conduct can create serious impediments to the cause of Christ. The principles listed above are especially important, as is the vision, which must be clearly defined and kept in focus.

> MED is a complex development strategy

Partnerships will be extremely useful, particularly for programs that face repayment difficulties due to expectations of Christian compassion, "kindness" and forgiveness (including loan forgiveness). Some efforts may be legally precluded from evangelism and discipleship, and will have to rely on lifestyle evangelism and partnering with national and international believers and ministries to achieve these outcomes.

There is clearly a need for more research on sound Christian MED practices in unreached areas in the 10-40 Window. World mission endeavors would benefit from learning more about programs operated by large Christian MED organizations and how they have been able to have an effective witness.

Incentives for effective spiritual transformation ministries

The MED industry has found that offering financial and other incentives to staff who do well in dispensing and collecting loans results in efficient financial performance of the program. The authors of this handbook believe that incentives should be provided to workers in Christian MED programs to encourage them in the spiritual dimension of their ministry. Financial revenue is not the only way to offer encouragement. Incentives can be a simple as:

- Praying for individual clients and for their salvation and spiritual growth;

- Praising field staff for work they do in evangelism and discipleship in addition to tasks related to loan transactions, e.g., publicizing staff initiative throughout the organization;

- Talking with field staff about their clients' spiritual lives and problems;

- Visiting local pastors.

Incentives for spiritual ministry should also be encouraged in the head offices of large international Christian MED networks. A second set of incentives for large Christian MED programs would be to devote resources and staff to studying and developing a set of "best practices" in

> *Incentives should be provided to workers in Christian MED programs to encourage them in the spiritual dimension of their ministry*

high impact spiritual ministries and publicize them to educate members of their network and other Christian MED organizations. Many Christian MED organizations have team members doing tremendous work with high holistic impact that need to be publicized for others to learn from.

Indicators of progress in spiritual transformation ministry

It is important to generate the indicators of desired developmental change and to regularly measure them. This will encourage team members to exert extra effort in weak areas. Christians are often afraid to use such indicators of spiritual ministries, out of distaste for reducing the work of the Holy Spirit to numerical exercises. Others hesitate because they believe that ultimately God calls Christians to be faithful whatever the growth may be. However, if Christian MED programs have holistic visions and objectives, they have no choice but to try and measure progress as part of a necessary action-reflection-action cycle of evaluating their work. They must have empirical data to reflect on.

Small MED programs which know their staff, clients, and local churches intimately are likely to have fewer problems with indicators than larger programs. Personnel in small programs can list each client and church and tell their story, outlining their progress and spiritual growth. However, once field staff begin serving several hundred people, while their supervisor manages staff

> *Christian MED programs have no choice but to measure progress*

serving thousands of clients, personal knowledge of clients diminishes. There is a danger that large MED programs may operate in the dark regarding the spiritual side of their work, and completely in the light on the financial side. Having a useful set of indicators for spiritual and social transformation helps shine the light on specific components.

All indicators, both financial and spiritual, must be relatively easy to measure if they are to be meaningful. The research conducted for this handbook did not reveal indicators of spiritual ministries that were regularly monitored. Group-based MED programs that have Christian group members should use focus groups or other strategies to gather quick and relatively reliable data to measure progress towards objectives. Similar focus group methods would also work well with local churches.

Costs and benefits of verbal proclaimation activities

The pioneering research of Llanto (1999) revealed that *verbal proclaimation activities, such as Bible studies, etc., would increase overhead costs by about 15% for the programs it researched.*[47] These organizations considered that this exercise would be an integral cost of conducting business.

With increased pressures on MED programs to strive towards financial self-sufficiency and compete for donor funds with other minimalist MED programs, it can be expected that intentional efforts at spiritual transformation may decrease. Should this occur, these programs must find Christian sources of funds for their holistic ministries or partner with other organizations or churches to provide non -financial services.

There is a need for research to measure how verbal proclaimation activities provide operational cost benefits for both clients and the organization to balance out expenses. Conversion and spiritual growth of clients and their families can result in changed lifestyles with better ability to repay loans on time, as well as increased leadership potential to encourage others to pay on time. The spiritual growth of staff can result in a higher sense of calling to the work, resulting in higher morale, commitment, and better performance. The verbal proclaimation of the gospel contains both costs and benefits which need to be measured.

> *With increased pressures on MED programs to strive towards financial self-sufficiency and compete for donor funds with other minimalist MED programs, it can be expected that intentional efforts at verbal proclaimation may decrease*

Check List of Crucial Spiritual Transformation Issues

☐ Staff must be *trained* for spiritual transformation activities.

☐ There must be strategies for the spiritual transformation of clients which includes evangelism, discipleship, and training in Biblical worldview.

☐ There must be effective *partnerships with other ministries* and churches that can help in the spiritual transformation work. It requires concerted efforts to strengthen partnerships so that clients are presented with a holistic gospel of Jesus Christ.

☐ The program must design strategies and articulate principles which will build up the *local church*. These must reflect the following:

- A strong understanding of the religious, socio-political, and economic contexts;
- Continuous emphasis of the imperative for high levels of stewardship and accountability to church leadership and clients;
- Avoids entangling the pastor in difficult MED program decisions;
- Savings mobilization which are used effectively to build stewardship and accountability, rather than relying solely on outside funds;
- Program design which assists the local church in developing strategies to help people survive emergencies; and
- Where outside funding is involved, structuring the program so that it maintains enough distance from the church to enforce loan repayment.

- [ ] There must be *incentives* to encourage spiritual transformation work by program staff.

- [ ] The program must be linked to *national and international networks* which develop incentives to encourage its implementing affiliates to conduct spiritual transformation activities.

- [ ] There must be *indicators* used to assess the progress of spiritual transformation within the organization, among the local churches, and clients.

- [ ] Verbal proclaimation activities must be viewed as having extremely high potential benefits to the organization.

CHAPTER 7

In this chapter . . .

This last chapter briefly discusses and reviews additional strategic issues for Christian MED programs to be effective. This includes: context, strategic partnerships, fraud, MIS systems, and issues on impact assessment, repayment and special issues for Christian MED.

Additional Strategic Issues

Understanding the context in which Christian MED programs operate

At several points in this handbook, contextual issues have been discussed. The *macro-economic environment* can create adverse preconditions for people to save and influences their decisions on how they use their finances. It also creates inflationary conditions that MED programs must manage in order to protect their loan portfolio from devaluation. The *socio-political context* impacts such rudimentary social values as trust and confidence. Countries in or emerging from civil war contexts have to rebuild community solidarity and trust necessary for group-based MED programs to be effective.

Tribalism is a factor to be addressed in almost every African MED program. Local and national politics make it extremely difficult for self-help groups to operate independently and to avoid interference or being co-opted by elites.

Chapter 4 demonstrates that MED programs clearly operate in contexts where people were already deploying *local contextual financial services* before the intervention of MED arrived. It is crucial that practitioners understand why people use these services and how they help or hurt them. Part of these services may be provided by other MED programs, including some that are extremely minimalist and focus only on financial services. Christian MED programs must design and implement their work in a unique way that does not damage these programs

> *Christian MED programs must design and implement their work in unique ways that do not damage these programs with unfair, subsidized competition that is not sustainable*

with unfair, subsidized competition that is not sustainable (that is, if they truly seek the long-term well-being of their clients).

The *cultural and religious context* has an important role in how Christian MED programs design their spiritual transformation activities. Implementing MED in Cambodia under anti-Christian governments, with funds from secular donors, requires creative strategies. It is very different from conducting MED in a Roman Catholic context such as the Philippines or Latin America.

The extreme variance of contexts makes it important to have partnerships and affiliations with like-minded organizations that can help a program provide or promote holistic services.

It is essential to belong to a support network where one can access training, education and support when necessary, and be held accountable for performance. This applies to mission- and church-led MED programs as well as MED programs implemented by Christian NGOs.

The current trend with large Christian MED organizations is to bring overseas affiliates into a network so they can benefit from technical services support and a greater degree of quality control. The OI Network has developed a standard methodological package (which it calls "Trust Banking") it provides this model to its partners to develop, adapt, and build

> *Fraud happens within client groups, between clients and staff, among staff, and even in top management and governance*

on. The Faulu MED programs of Food for the Hungry International in East Africa also operate in this manner and provide consistent high quality MIS, finance, reporting, and other systems. World Relief and others are moving in this direction.

Minimizing the risk of fraud

Minimizing fraud is essentially a discipline of holding people accountable through adequate management and MIS. Accountability for all members of the board of directors, staff and clients is extremely crucial in MED programs of all sizes, because people, Christians included, are sinful.

Fraud happens within client groups, between clients and staff, among staff, and even in top management and governance. It can penetrate every part of an organization. At the delivery and transaction levels, complete transparency in financial dealings between the program

> *It is not uncommon for staff to find ways to defraud the organization. One common strategy is for field staff to invent "ghost" clients or "ghost" groups/banks and pocket the money*

and the clients helps control fraud by clients or staff. At the client level, it is imperative that all financial transactions are signed by as many clients/members as possible, and that all funds move openly in front of other people. This also helps protect the program from "special exclusive relationships" between staff and clients where money may flow to staff in order for loans to be made.[48]

It is not uncommon for staff to find ways to defraud the organization. One common strategy is for field staff to invent "ghost" clients or "ghost" groups/banks and pocket the money. This type of fraud can best be minimized by internal audits in which management routinely checks the validity of clients and groups served by the program. Another strategy is for staff to divert loan repayments made by clients. This can be controlled by *providing clients with passbooks* which they use to keep track of their own repayments, by *using internal audits* where clients are visited, and by *having an MIS that keeps track of loan payments* on a timely basis.

Top management can also be involved in fraud. In such situations, regular outside audits are needed, as well as strong governance to verify management practices and hold top management accountable. Unfortunately, accountability structures come with a price that escalates as the program grows. Monitoring two field staff and several hundred clients is much easier and cheaper than monitoring large numbers of field staff and 20,000 clients. Size inevitably increases complexity.

One way to minimize fraud is to maintain detailed statistical reports. But the more detailed the statistic, the more expensive to collect and process accurate data. Christian MED programs must aggressively identify and install the most efficient fraud control tools available, such as a code of ethics, transparency, dispensing loans by cheques, etc., and deploy these where appropriate.[49]

MIS explained

Accurate information is crucial in MED. Validated information must guide decision-making processes and actions. *Timely and accurate information helps MED programs serve people more effectively and efficiently.* It is useful in monitoring staff and clients, and in identifying areas that require special attention. When Citicorp made a recent series of small grants to North American MED programs, 6 of the 10 proposals it funded were for MIS development. *MIS is "the series of processes and actions*

> *Validated information must guide the decision-making process as the basis for action*

involved in capturing raw data, processing the data into usable information, and disseminating the information in the form needed."[50] MIS is not just a computer or software program. It is everything that happens to track data about a $2 loan payment made by a tomato seller as the data moves through the system and is processed into accurate reports for management and loan officers in the field. MIS includes both portfolio tracking (savings and loans) and accounting information (such as income and expenses). Large MED programs require the following sets of reports from their MIS on a monthly basis:[51]

- The *portfolio report* describes portfolio quality as measured by arrears rates and efficiency variables such as client and portfolio per loan officer, etc. This monitors the health of the MED program's "investments" in loans to the poor.

- The *balance sheet* summarizes the organization's sources and uses of funds. It is critical to know where the program has invested its capital and how well it is performing.

- The *income (profit and loss) statement* shows how the program is performing in covering its costs and how much, if any, subsidy it requires to continue.

- The *cash flow statement* reports the program's cash position and its ability to transact loans. This is essential because lack of cash can damage a program's incentives for repayment and slow down its growth.

The authors believe that these MIS reports are equally important for small MED programs as they are for large organizations. Smaller programs, however, would not need them as frequently as larger programs.[52] Small MED programs can use simple systems to gather and store data, and create reports. For those with relatively few clients and a small portfolio, adequate reporting can be achieved by simple ledger accounting systems.

As MED programs increase in size, it becomes vital that they invest in MIS. Poor information will kill a MED program very quickly. Rapid growth also necessitates the development of administrative systems and training programs to manage the increasing number of employees.

Assessing program impact

Designing effective impact measurement systems is an aspect that many MED programs struggle with. Most Christian MED programs seek to facilitate holistic change. Almost all rely on anecdotal stories to demonstrate that they are achieving high impact. This practice is generally adequate for public relations and supporters, but Biblical accountability requires all stakeholders not to be content with mere anecdotes of impact. Findings based on real data are much more valuable.

> *Biblical accountability requires all stakeholders not to be content with mere anecdotes of impact*

The secular MED industry contends that it is too expensive and methodologically difficult to accurately measure impact on clients. While there are certainly barriers to accurate impact assessment, smaller programs are free to be creative since they usually know their clients personally.

Larger programs can take two approaches to assess their developmental impact:

1. Conduct periodic studies.
2. Develop systems to measure impact on a regular basis.

Periodic studies can reveal interesting findings about impact that enable a MED program to improve its services. But regular impact monitoring is even more powerful. The frontier of impact assessment is in two areas:

- Gathering impact data through regular MIS-produced reports
- Using participatory strategies to assess impact with clients

MIS-generated impact assessments provide detailed reports, but they reflect mainly surface level impacts such as enterprise characteristics, loan size trajectory, repayment history, etc. Participatory approaches can provide insight on how the program affected clients' decisions. This can be extremely useful, particularly when combined with MIS-generated reports. Impact assessment is expensive and most MED programs lack the skills to do it well. This is an area where members of Christian MED networks could jointly develop and disseminate appropriate impact assessment

> *Christian MED networks could jointly develop and disseminate appropriate impact assessment methodologies, and train practitioners on their use*

methodologies, and train practitioners on their use.

Avoiding repayment crisis

People are sinful and their sinful choices result in periodic crises. Structural evil and sin also stimulate economic conditions that engender repayment crises. Consequently, *almost every MED program experiences a repayment crisis at some time, during which it would seem that the program is melting down.* In such situations, it is important to monitor the manner in which the organization responds. Available MED literature on repayment crises is fairly limited at the time of writing. This accentuates the need to warn that unchecked repayment crises spread rapidly and can infect an entire program within a short period. The confidence of clients, staff, and donors in the program plummets, exacerbating loan recovery.

World Relief Cambodia brought in consultants to help resolve their repayment crisis. The lessons they learned are as follows:

- *Admit the problem* and source external help.
- *Change* the organizational *culture*.
- *Establish fire-fighting teams* to identify problems, meet with each delinquent client, and take action.
- *Engage all personnel* to focus efforts on addressing the problems.
- *Analyze the portfolio* to look for the trends which caused the crisis. Install adequate *management and MIS* to help supervise field workers.
- *Make loan amounts small* within village bank programs.

Dangers of market saturation

There are growing concerns that the MED market may soon be saturated with more finance providers than the market can bear. There is evidence that clients take loans from multiple MED programs in order to repay loans to another. This does not generally result in increased productive capacity at the enterprise level and, eventually, clients experience repayment problems and default. While organizations have for many years discussed the development of a joint data base to control this practice, it is unlikely until the risks exceed the benefits gained by attracting clients from other programs.

Major secular donors do not seem overly concerned about market saturation because one objective is to use the MED "market" to shake out the weaker players. They view the competition developing among MFIs as an advantage for clients

There are growing concerns that MED market may soon be saturated with more finance providers than the market can bear

because it will tend to keep costs lower, the assumption is that there is limited collusion between competing MFIs.

It is likely that the coming years will see a shaking out in the MED industry as the smaller, less efficient MFIs as well as the more holistic (and costly) programs loose their ability to compete with the larger minimalist MFIs for donor (and investor) funds. To survive, the smaller and more holistic MFIs may be forced to merge with larger, more efficient programs.

An emerging player in the informal finance sector is the formal banking houses. There is evidence that they are driving down their loan activities and products to attract the business of the poor. This segment of society previously viewed as unbankable are now receiving attention. Formal banks are significantly capitalized and could be a serious threat to informal finance providers.

> *To survive, the smaller and more holistic MFIs may be forced to merge with larger, more efficient programs*

For Christian players in the microfinance arena, it is imperative that their uniqueness and God given vision drives them to excell and survive against aggressive competition.

Check List of Crucial Strategic Issues

☐ The organization must adapt its programs to the local context.

☐ *The organization's leaders should recognize deficiencies* and adjust methodologies for a better fit.

☐ *The organization must partner with local organizations* to help carry out holistic mission.

☐ *The organization must partner with other MED organizations* to receive support and training and to keep the organization accountable to sound MED practices.

☐ The organization's leaders must consider joining an *MED network* and thereby benefit from the network's support.

☐ The organization should take measures to control potential *fraud*.

☐ The organization must recognize the need for timely, accurate *reporting* in the following areas:
  • Portfolio reports
  • Cash flow statements
  • Income statements
  • Balance sheets

☐ The organization must establish *MIS systems* that deliver accurate reports of key operational areas on a regular timely basis.

☐ The organization must assess *impact* in ways other than anecdotal stories.

☐ A strategy must be formulated to manage *repayment crises* when they occur.

☐ The organization must be aware of trends in increasing *market saturation* and its impact.

Executive Summary

The objective of this handbook was to provide information to help Christian MED practitioners and donors better *understand how to apply Christian MED in ways that build Christ's kingdom*. The handbook draws from literature on secular MED and eight case studies of Christian MED programs from around the world. It then compared the findings from both to identify the strengths and weaknesses of Christian MED.

1.   The eight Christian MED programs selected for the case studies are from the following organizations:
   * *Local Enterprise Assistance Program (LEAP)* of the Association of Evangelicals of Liberia;
   * *Sinapi Aba Trust (SAT)*, an Opportunity International affiliate in Ghana;
   * *Fondo de Inversiones Para el Desarollo de la Microempresa (FIME)*, a World Vision International lending program in the Dominican Republic;
   * *Center for Promotion of Andean Development (AYNI)* loan program in Peru, an upland Presbyterian church organization;
   * *Cambodian Community Building (CCB)*, a World Relief affiliate;
   * *Ventures and Entrepreneurship and Development Center in the Orient, Inc. (VEDCOR)*, a church-based savings and credit cooperative in the Philippines;
   * *Project Love in a Family Environment (L.I.F.E).* Foundation in Thai-

land, a YWAM missionary program on the Thai/Cambodian border; and

- *Center for Community Transformation (CCT)*, an Opportunity International affiliate in Manila.

2. The handbook focused on numerous important issues in Christian MED: vision and mission, MED methodologies, financial performance, leadership and governance, spiritual transformation activities and other strategic issues.

Vision and Mission

3. Vision is important to Christian MED programs because secular donors and sustainability standards drive much of the MED "industry", creating tensions between spiritual transformation activities and program sustainability. There are six important elements of vision for Christian MED:

    (a)   *vision for development* – Christian *development* requires the following:

- belief in the necessity for a personal relationship with Jesus Christ;
- a Biblical worldview;
- focus on both the global and local Church;
- integral development of people; and
- understanding of the multi-dimensional nature of deprivation.

    (b)   *vision for sustainability* – Sustainability requires balancing a "healthy tension" between strengthening the structures, systems and funding necessary for sustainability with the focus on providing transformational lending for the poor.

(c)   *vision for the local church* – An effective Christian MED program works in partnership with other CDOs where in strategies for strengthening the local church are formulated.

(d)   *marketing vision* – While praiseworthy, Christian MED programs that rely on secular MED donors must recognize the impediments and implications of promoting their intentional spiritual goals. Explicit declarations of intent can lead to reduced funding from secular sources. In areas that restrict evangelism, Christian MED programs may need to be more circumspect in their promotions.

(e)   *time and funding commitment* – Christian MED requires a long-term commitment to reduce the risks of microfinance to their beneficiaries, the local church, and to the credit culture. The time commitment varies depending on whether an organization is providing or promoting MED services.

(f)   *sustaining the vision* – Mission drift in Christian MED can be avoided if the mission is communicated to all, its impact is measured, and clients participate in critical program decisions.

MED Methodologies

4.   *Clear targeting* of beneficiaries is critical because methodologies

that work for the very poor at the income-generating level may not work for small enterprises. Christian MED practitioners need to understand the "best practices" of MED within the niche they serve.

5. Christian MED practitioners need to understand the importance of *savings* and must be capable of designing creative savings services. *Informal finance* mechanisms can teach Christian MED programs how to be more effective in their particular area.

6. Negative effects of *bad microfinance* programs can damage informal credit systems, credit cultures and local churches. These effects should be avoided through clear and effective strategies to enforce loan repayment.

7. It is important for Christian MED practitioners to understand the differences between *providing, promoting and partnering* in MED in terms of the time commitment, sustainability issues, types of services, goals, linkages required, and macro-economic and political conditions. For example, in terms of sustainability, providers of MED (i.e., those that actually operate a MED program) need to generate their own long-term sources of financing rather than rely on outside subsidy. In contrast, outside subsidy may be permissible for MED organizations that only do promotional work, at least at the beginning.

8. To be able to choose strategies that best alleviate poverty, Christian MED practitioners need to know the chief design principles of the

different MED lending methodologies. Special knowledge of the risks in agricultural production and the informal agri-credit market is required for agricultural lending.

Financial Performance

9.   While Christian MED organizations must be aware of the dangers of making financial sustainability the main goal of their programs, they must also know the determinants of a financially sound MED program. Christian MED practitioners must understand both the supply and demand aspects and variables of their *market.*

10. *Accurate financial indicators* such as portfolio quality, sustainability ratios, and efficiency indicators are critical to measuring performance and ensuring program effectiveness and efficiency. Ensuring *on-time repayment* is critical to survival and requires proper management of default through measurement of the portfolio-at-risk and periodic writing-off of bad loans.

11. Maintenance and accurate estimation of an *adequate capital base* is necessary to ensure the sustainability of a loan program. Clients who are not assured of a follow-up loan will not have an incentive to repay their current loans.

12. While subsidies may be permissible during the start-up of a program, these should not be used to hide inefficiency.

     Subsidy is better applied to start-up costs, expansion, piloting experiments and other transformation services rather than for financial components of a MED program. Interest and fees from users of the financial services should eventually fund all finance-related elements of a MED program. Ascertaining the correct interest rate is the most critical aspect of ensuring the sustainability of a MED program.

13. Best practice in secular MED requires programs to aim for both operational *self-sufficiency* (this includes covering salaries, other operational and administrative expenses, interest fees, and loan loss provisions) and *financial self-sufficiency* (imputing costs of inflation and grants). Since it is estimated that verbal proclaimation activities add up to 15 % to operational costs, a Christian MED program must determine the extent and function subsidies will play in its funding strategy.

14. While *borrowing funds* to support loan operations is part of best practice for MFIs, Christian MED practitioners must be sure that the conditions of these loans do not limit their vision and objectives.

15. Critical *efficiency measurements* include number of clients per loan officer (best practice is 200-400), value of portfolio loan per officer, and delivery cost per dollar within loan portfolios.

Leadership and Governance

16. While a capable executive director is critical for success, *oversight*

and accountability occur through boards of directors of secular MED programs. *Mature Christian leadership* at the board and management levels are needed to balance aims for financial self-sufficiency and kingdom-building. Governing authorities must provide direction in the following areas: achieving vision, legal obligations, strategic directions, fiduciary oversight, self-assessment and renewal and oversight of the program.

17. *Nationals* are more effective in the long run at managing and governing local MED programs. *Effective governance* at the board level requires the provision of continuity of leadership, having knowledge of the local MED industry and successfully adapting to it, effecting change in management strategies and styles to suit the different stages of organizational maturity.

18. As an oversight structure, boards are expected to formulate policies which would:
    - embody the values and priorities of the board & stake holders,
    - operate as guidelines and parameters for management, and
    - provide a framework for decision-making both for the board and management.

Spiritual Transformation Activities

19. To be effective, a Christian MED organization must:
    (a) be led by the Holy Spirit,
    (b) implement strategies for spiritual formation, and

(c) implement strategies for equipping the local church.

To ensure effectiveness, it is necessary to encourage the *spiritual development of the organizations personnel* in order to create holistic impact on clients. Organizations must decide as to whether they will train their own personnel to engage in evangelism or form strategic alliances with external specialist groups.

20. Proper selection of loan methodologies can enhance spiritual impact on clients. There is some evidence that group-based methodologies could have higher impact in social and spiritual areas than individual-based loan programs.

21. To be able to strengthen the *local church*, a Christian MED organization must:
    (a) Know its context well,
    (b) Provide systems to ensure stewardship and accountability,
    (c) Prohibit pastors from making or influencing decisions on loans,
    (d) Focus on savings mobilization for capital build-up,
    (e) Provide insurance schemes for emergencies,
    (f) Structure the program to have a "para-church" identity in the community, and
    (g) Find partners to help equip the local church.

22. Christian MED programs must provide *non-financial incentives* to encourage staff in their spiritual ministry. Accurate indicators are critical in spiritual transformation work. Further research is needed

to measure how verbal proclaimation of the gospel provide benefits for both clients and personnel with cost effective results.

Additional Strategic Issues

23. Smaller Christian MED programs benefit from linkages with larger networks in order to obtain technical services and ensuring quality control.

24. To minimize *fraud* it is advisable:
    a. to have client passbooks,
    b. use internal audits where clients are visited, and
    c. to track loans through an effective Management Information System (MIS).

25. Appropriate impact assessment methodologies for Christian MED programs need to be developed.

26. Almost every MED program will experience a *repayment crisis*. A comprehensive strategy is needed to manage this when it happens.

27. Developing a joint client database is one solution proposed to handle the issue of MED saturation. Although secular MED organizations believe that increased competition will lead to greater efficiency in the microfinance industry.

28. Christian MED is more difficult than secular MED because it seeks to provide more than mere microfinance services. While Christian

MED strives to transform people's lives, build God's kingdom, and equip the local church, when done badly it can result in irreversible damage.

29. The issues raised in this summary serve to provide pointers for Christian MED implementers who wish to give of their best to the Master.

Glossary of Technical Terms used in the Handbook

1. **2/3 World** – countries also known as the Third World, Low-Income Countries or Developing Countries. the use of "2/3" indicates that they constitute about 2/3 of the world's population.

2. **10/40 Window** – the regions between 10 degrees North and 40 degrees North, where 95% of the world's least evangelized poor are found (AD2000 and Beyond Movement).

3. **Delinquency** – Refers to loan payments which are past due. Also referred to as Arrears. (Source: Philippine Coalition for Microfinance Standards)

4. **Equity** – also referred to as Net Worth, Fund Balance or Net Assets. Equal to the assets less the organization's liabilities. Unlike liabilities, the equity of an organization does not have to be repaid. It therefore represents the value of the organization. Equity might include capital contributions of investors or donors, retained earnings, and current year surplus. Average Equity can be calculated by taking the value of equity at the first date of the period, adding the value of equity at the last date of the period, and dividing the sum by two. (Source: Philippine Coalition for Microfinance Standards)

5. **Financial Self-Sufficiency** – indicates whether sufficient revenue is earned to cover all the operating, financial and loan loss expenses as well as maintaining the value of the assets in the organization including

inflation.

6. **Formal Finance** – regulated financial activities, such as banks, regulated credit unions and cooperatives, legal pawnshops, insurance companies, etc.

7. **Informal finance** – all financial transactions and activities, e.g., loans, deposits, insurance, etc. occurring outside the jurisdiction of central financial regulatory authorities.

8. **Leverage** – the ability of the institution to expand available resources by borrowing against its equity. (Source: Philippine Coalition for Microfinance Standards)

9. **Liabilities** – represent what is owed by the organization to others. Average liabilities can be calculated by taking the total liabilities at the first date of the period, adding the total liabilities at the last date of the period, and dividing the sum by two. Current or Short-Term Liabilities refer to the outstanding amounts that the organization owes to banks, other creditors, or clients which are due to be repaid within one year. (Source: Philippine Coalition for Microfinance Standards)

10. **Liquidity** – the ability to meet demands for cash and current obligations as they become due. (Source: Philippine Coalition for Microfinance Standards)

11. **Loan Portfolio** – total principal value of outstanding loans (current, past due and restructured loans) receivable at a specific date. (Also referred to as Loans Outstanding, Active Portfolio or Loans Receivable). Average Loan Portfolio or Average Loans Outstanding is the average

value of total loans outstanding over a period. Average outstanding balance can be calculated by taking the opening balance of loans outstanding at the last date of the period, and dividing the sum by two. (Also referred to as Average Loans Receivable). (Source: Philippine Coalition for Microfinance Standards)

12. **Loan Term** – period of time over which a loan is to be repaid. Also known as Repayment Period/Term of the Loan. (Source: Philippine Coalition for Microfinance Standards)

13. **Management Information System (MIS)** – the series of process and actions involved in capturing raw data, processing the data into usable information and disseminating the information in the form needed.

14. **Microenterprise Development (MED)** – a developmental strategy that provides a broad package of financial services (savings, credit, insurance) as well as other business development services (business training, marketing assistance, etc.) to entrepreneurs to enable them to operate their own productive economic activities.

15. **Microfinance** – this is a component of MED involving savings, credit and insurance services.

16. **Operating Expense/Cost** – expenses which are related to the management of the loan fund. For a single-purpose microfinancial institution, it includes all costs. For multi-purpose institutions, includes all direct costs of micro-financial operations and an appropriate portion of the institution's overhead. Includes: loan loss provision, personnel and

administrative expense, financial cost such as interest and fee expenses. (Source: Philippine Coalition for Microfinance Standards)

17. **Operating Self-Sufficiency** – indicates whether adequate revenue has been generated to cover an organization's outgoing, including operational costs, loan loss provision, etc.

18. **Past Due** – loans with at least one missed amortization. (Source: Philippine Coalition for Microfinance Standards)

19. **Personnel Expense** – amount earned by staff for services rendered. Includes salaries, wages, benefits, etc. (Source: Philippine Coalition for Microfinance Standards)

20. **Portfolio at Risk** – banking concept based on the assumption that loans with late payments are at higher risk of default. It is calculated by the value of loans outstanding in which payments late over a given time period divided by the total value of all loans outstanding.

21. **Principal Amount of the Loan** – the face or stated amount of the loan upon which interest is calculated. Outstanding principal is the amount owed by the borrower at any time, excluding interest. (Source: Philippine Coalition for Microfinance Standards)

22. **Trust Banks** – the new name used by the OI Network members for Village Banks; a group lending methodolgy that targets the poorest of the economically active population. 15 to 40 members are self-selected so they can access loans for non-farming, income-generating activities.

23. **Village Banks** – village level organizations that provide microfinance services such as credit and savings so the poor can access such

services. A group lending methodolgy that targets the poorest of the economically active population and requires them to save prior to receiving loans. 15 to 40 members are self-selected so they can access loans for non-farming, income-generating activities. Village bank loans do not require collateral but members are expected to co-guarantee all loans and make weekly payments to their village bank.

Foreword

1   Discipling A Whole Nation (DAWN) reports founded in 1985. Dawn serves the Body of Christ in 148 nations to see a church within easy access of every person.

Chapter 1

2   A consultation held in Dana Point, Orange County, USA, attended by 16 Christian donor and implementing organizations to discuss the emerging prominence of Christian MED and the proliferation of requests received by donors for funds.

Chapter 2

3   See Keller, T.J., (1997), Ministries of Mercy, The Call of the Jericho Road; Miller, D.L. & Guthrie, S. (1998), Discipling Nations: The Power of Truth to Transform Cultures; Myers, B. (1999), Walking with the Poor: Principles and Practices of Transformational Development; Sider, R. (1997), Rich Christians in an Age of Hunger: Moving from Affluence to Generosity; and Chambers, R. (1983), Rural Development: Putting the Last First.

4   Fears of alienating secular donors led this Christian organization to use this definition in its publication.

5   Waterfield, C. & Duval, A. (1996), p. 11.

6   Characteristics of an effective CMED program as discussed in the Dana Point Consultation, Annex.

7   KMBI's portfolio was too large for it to be included in this research.

8   This is particularly true in countries where no credit rating agency exists of where loan clients are not included in credit rating systems.

Chapter 3

9   Adapted from Waterfield and Duval (1996), Care Savings and Credit Sourcebook. Waterfield worked for many years with MEDA in Haiti and also directed CARE's MED department.

9a   For example, missions promotional materials for the 10-40 Window say that 85%

or more of the world's "poorest of the poor" live in the 10-40 Window. But they seldom define what that means.

10   There are many good books on savings and informal financial savings systems, e.g. see Johnson S. and Rogaly, B. (1997), Microfinance and Poverty Reduction, for a brief summary and Von Pischke, J.D. (1991), Finance as the Frontier: Debt Capacity and the Role of Credit in the Private Economy for an in-depth discussion of theory and practice.

11   A good academic work on informal finance is Adams, D.W. and Fitchet, D.A. (1992), Informal Finance in Low-Income Countries.

12   Rutherford (1999), The Poor and their Money: an Essay about Financial Services for Poor People, p. 18.

13   Bouman, F.J.A. and Moll, H.A.J. (1992), Informal Finance in Indonesia, p. 222.

14   Ardener, S. & Burman, S. (1995), Money-go-rounds: The Importance of Rotating Savings and Credit Associations for Women., p. 13.

15   Rutherford (1999), The Poor and their Money: an Essay about Financial Services for People, p. 18.

16   See Waterfield, C. & Duval, A. (1996), Care Savings & Credit Sourcebook, pp. 79-130 & ibid for fuller discussions of MED methodologies.

17   Rutherford (1999), The Poor and their Money: an Essay about Financial Services for Poor People, p. 18.

18   Ibid.

19   See Adams, D.W. & Fitchett, D.A. (1992), Informal Finance in Low Income Countries, for detailed research on failed government finance.

20   Evidence from the Gambia is that providing outside loans to ROSCAs encouraged them to gradually exclude the poorer members.

21   Senior claims are "obligations that the borrower considers more important than repaying the lender." Vpn Pischke, J.D., (1994), Structuring Credit to Manager Real Risks.

Chapter 4

22   Waterfield, C. & Duval, A. (1996), p. 3.

23   Particularly regarding the integrity and security if clients' deposits/savings.

24   Johnson, S. and Rogaly, B. (1997), Microfinance and Poverty Reduction, pp. 27-28.

25   SEEP Network 1995 for example.

26     $\dfrac{\text{Total Cost}}{\text{Loan Portfolio}}$ See SEEP Network 1995 literature

27   Example: Three loans are 35 days in arrears and their outstanding balance is $10,000. The total value of all loans outstanding (also called loan portfolio) is $100,000. Thus, the 30-day portfolio at risk rate is 10%.

28   See Von Pischke, J.V.D. (1991), Finance at the Frontier: Debt Capacity and the Role of Credit in the Private Economy, for a thorough discussion of the components of finance.

29   Grameen Bank generally stays "awash in cash" as a way to cope with Bangladesh's regular cyclones and massive flooding.

30   Time Frame is important. A microfinance program is more likely to cover costs after 5 years than in year one.

31   OSS is calculated as follows: all financial income (interest, fees, income from investments) divided by financial costs plus operating costs plus loan loss provision.

32   See the SEEP Network's Financial Ratio Analysis of Microfinance Institutions for more details.

33   Llanto's work is groundbreaking and should be followed by similar research in other contexts that read Gilbert's paper and modify to include counterveiling cost reduction potentials as well.

34   "Best Practices" microfinance also calls for savings mobilization as a base for loan capital – when appropriately regulated by national banking laws and institutions.

35   CCB took a stealthy approach and built their credibility through quality MED, and is now beginning to institutionalize in their transformation activities.

36   See Burbank, K. (1999) for more thorough discussion of interest.

37   Results of a comparative study of 11 MFI programs around the world (Christen et. al. 1995, p. 31).

Chapter 5

38   Rock, R., Otero, M. & Saltzman, S., (1998), Principles and Practices of Microfinance Governance, p. 1.

39   CCB was still determining an appropriate ownership structure in light of Cambodia's rapidly changing regulatory framework.

40   Governing bodies may be referred to in different ways depending on the legal status of the organization, i.e., Board of Directors, Board of Trustees, Board of Governors, etc.

41   Campion and Frankiewicz 1999.

42   Carver, J., (1990), Boards that Make a Difference.

43   Rhyne, E. and Rotblatt, L.S., (1994), What Makes them Tick? Exploring the Anatomy of Major Microenterprise Finance Organizations.

Chapter 6

44   This question occurs with some regularity in Cambodia among CCB field staff.

45   Partnering organizations like Interdev may be helpful in selecting partners.

46   In some cultures, local money is considered "hotmoney" that is to be handled with care. Outside money or "cold money" does not attract the same degree of stewardship.

47   The cost occurred primarily through time allocated to spiritual ministries by staff and expenses related to those activities.

Chapter 7

48   Russell Mask observed this happening even among church members in a MED program in the Philippines.

49   See Rhyne, E. and Rotblatt, L.S. (1994), What Makes them Tick? Exploring the Anatomy of Major Microenterprise Finance Organizations, for more discussion of fraud control methods.

50   Waterfield, C. and Ramsing, N. (1998), Handbook for Management Information Systems for MFIs, p. 3.

51   See SEEP (1995) for a clear discussion of financial ratios.

52   Balance sheets and income statements may not be necessary for small programs except on an annual basis. Portfolio reports and cash flow statements are, however, extremely important on monthly or weekly basis.

Research Methodology

The research which accompanies this Handbook identified and studied eight case studies of Christian organizations doing MED, and draws on the data gathered from those cases. The cases were determined using the following selection criteria:

1. Two to three cases in each 2/3 World region (Asia, Africa, Latin America)

2. Christian MED programs with the following criteria:

- Staffed by Christians at management level and at most field staff levels;

- Kept the local church in focus at least as a partner in holistic ministry;

- Had a vision of Biblical transformation that includes the desire of clients to have a saving knowledge and a relationship with Jesus Christ, growing in their faith, and adopting a Biblical worldview;

- Regularly measured results in its spiritual ministries;

- Ensured post-loan nurturing of clients even after they exit the MED program (CDOs, partner ministries, church, etc.).

3. Interfaced and collaborated with other CDOs.

4. Targeted the poor, if not exclusively, at least in terms of numbers of clients.

5. Was on a path to cover Program costs through revenues generated by MED activities.

6. Had a loan portfolio (outstanding loan balance) of US$50,000-$500,000.

7. Has clear accountability/governing structures (for programs in the $500,000 range).

8. Has been operating for a minimum of 3 years.

9. Has the following number of clients (for direct implementers):
   - 500 active clients or more for $50,000–$99,999 programs;
   - 1,000 clients or more for $100,000–$299,999 programs;
   - 2,000 clients or more for $300,000 or larger programs.

Introductory letters were mailed to the CEOs of all major Christian Relief and Development Organizations, MED network and donor organizations describing the research. The researchers requested recommendations for top quality programs that seek to be cost-covering and have intentional kingdom impact.

The following cases were selected for field research:
- *Local Enterprise Assistance Program (LEAP)* of the Association of

Evangelicals of Liberia;

- *Sinapi Aba Trust (SAT)*, an Opportunity International affiliate in Ghana;
- *Fondo de Inversiones Para el Desarollo de la Microempresa (FIME)*, a World Vision International lending program in the Dominican Republic;
- *Center for Promotion of Andean Development (AYNI)* loan program in Peru, an upland Presbyterian church organization;
- *World Relief Cambodia (WR/C)*
- *Ventures and Entrepreneurship and Development Center in the Orient, Inc. (VEDCOR)*, a church-based savings and credit cooperative in the Philippines;
- *Project Love in a Family Environment (L.I.F.E).* Foundation in Thailand, a YWAM missionary program on the Thai/Cambodian border; and
- *Center for Community Transformation (CCT)*, an Opportunity International affiliate in Manila.

Refer to Tables 4 & 5

Data Gathering

The authors designed the questionnaire in consultation with other Christian MED staff, particularly the staff of World Relief. Several reknown Christian MED workers commented on the questionnaires.

Outside researchers were hired to cover five of the seven cases selected. All were professing Christians who had been involved in Christian MED work in various capacities for a number of years. Three were North Americans, two were Asian. One of the authors of this handbook, Russell Mask, personally did the field research for two of the cases. One of the cases, LEAP, was studied by researchers from the parent MED network. While using relative insiders

The case study survey questions are available on request. You may contact the CMED Secretariat at cmed@info.com.ph

could impact objectivity, it allowed greater transparency since credibility had already been established. The field visits were five days except in the case of Project L.I.F.E., which was three days.

The following are the sources of data used for the research:

- Organizational records (reports, evaluations, profit and loss statements, balance sheets, case studies, stories, etc.);
- Interviews with members of the board of directors or advisors, management, field staff, clients and pastors.

Analysis and Writing

The researchers who completed the field research were responsible for writing the cases. Russell Mask did the initial analysis and summary of the cases and presented the results at the Christian MED Summit in Thailand in May 1999. David Bussau reviewed the findings, provided the framework for the analysis and assessed the relevance of the data. Final analysis and writing for this handbook was completed in the fourth quarter of 1999 after the remaining cases were completed.

Updating and Revisions

The MED field is fluid and dynamic. The best practices of today will be improved tomorrow. The authors welcome comments, case studies and tips about other Christian MED programs that have been effective at spiritual transformation while striving for sustainability so that future literature on Christian MED can reflect the most sound.

Characteristics of an Effective CMED Organization

1. Spiritually Focused
   a. It has an intentional strategy to see that planting, growing and strengthening the local church occur;
   b. There is a passion and strategies for spiritual transformation, personal and cultural;
   c. It involves the local church;
   d. Holy Spirit based prayer is a priority to the leadership.

2. Strong Leadership
   a. The organization is directed by strong governance, that is vision driven, focused and respectful of the different roles of board and management;
   b. It has trained, competent personnel who are solidly Christian;
   c. There is substantial indigenous representation;
   d. The leadership exhibits integrity, trust, self-confidence accountability, teachability, and flexibility –not fear change;
   e. The organization is concerned with continuity and servant leadership development.

3. Values Based
   a. There is a willingness and ability to partner;
   b. It satisfied needs of stakeholders;
   c. The organization and programs are biblically based;

d. A core value is serving the poor:
1. by training and equipping;
2. through family enhancing programs ;
3. by being culturally sensitive;
e. A commitment to promoting and verifying its values is demonstrated.

4. Results sensitive
   a. Leadership exhibits a desire to honestly measure and evaluate:
   1. spiritual indicators, including church health;
   2. financial results;
   3. change in client welfare;
   4. organizational health;
   5. change in social impact in the community;
   6. movement towards a biblical world view.
   b. An openness to change based on what is measured.

5. Financially Sound
   a. There is a large enough initial capital base;
   b. The issue of "financial viability" (B/E after all costs) is clearly addressed;
   c. There are good repayment rates;
   d. The organization's leadership understands the market;
   e. There is prudence in making decision on leveraging;
   f. An appropriate system is in place to discourage corruption;
   g. Definition and standards of accountability that are articulated, taught, measured and reported are in place.

Tables

Table 1: Vision in Christian Microenterprise Development

Indicator	Case Studies	Secular MED Standards and Trends
Vision for Development	Generally Holistic. Variability in understanding that the local church is necessary. Biblical worldview was not part of the development vision of any program.	The Minimalist Model is the current trend. The development needs of the poor are very broad. Microfinance can only meet part of people's needs. To do MED effectively and sustainably, MED programs should focus only on microfinance products.
Vision for Sustainability	Four of the sample cases had a vision for full financial self-sufficiency (SAT, WR/C, LEAP, and FIME). VEDCOR was funded by grants from a mother church and sought sustainability for its savings and credit cooperatives. AYNI had a mixed vision because of different development services. Its concern for cost-covering grew when its survival became at risk. Project L.I.F.E. seemed to have little notion of sustainability funded by income from borrowers and was still heavily reliant on outside grants and missionary funds.	Financial self-sufficiency is the bottom line. All operational and financial costs of the services must be covered by interest and fees paid by the clients and in income from investments. External subsidies are to be avoided after 3-5 years.
Vision for the Local Church	Six of the case studies (VEDCOR, LEAP, SAT, FIME, AYNI and Project L.I.F.E.) had great concern for the local church with a clear vision to help build it up through MED. WR/C itself was not well focused on the local church, although its parent, World Relief, had clear strategies for placing overlapping services (including church planting) in areas where WR/C operated.	No concern with the local church or other local institutions except for their usefulness for achieving high rates of on-time loan repayment and sustainability of the MED program.
Marketing Vision	WR/C was very careful about Christian identity because of the hostile context. SAT was cautious with donors because of secular funding. All other programs were more explicitly Christian in their promotional materials.	Microfinance programs need to be clear that they promote themselves as providing financial services that can stimulate either economic development or poverty alleviation, but not always both. Religion can be relevant for motivation as long as there is no discrimination.
Time and Funding Commitment	All case studies were started up with long-term intentions. The funding cycles varied in WR/C, which enforced secular donor requirements on the organization.	Sustainability requires a long-term focus. Start-up subsidy is acceptable for MED programs but they should seek to replace external grants with equity investments and loans accessed from local capital markets.
Sustaining Vision	SAT was very strong on maintaining vision through staff commitment, impact measurement and board involvement. VEDCOR had strong board involvement with vision. AYNI has had movement in its vision. WR/C was moving forward in kingdom building in a hostile context.	Communicate and inculcate vision, take time for reflection, measure impact, involve clients

Note: Current as of May 1999

Table 2: Key Characteristics of Basic MED Lending Methodologies

Principles	Individual Lending	Latin American Solidarity Group Lending	Grameen Banking	Village Banking	Community-Managed Revolving Loan Fund	Savings and Credit Cooperative/ Credit Union
Clients	Individual businesses often above poverty line	Individual businesses of people at or above poverty line	Individual members or groups of people often well below poverty line	Groups of people usually well below poverty line	Groups of members with mixed poverty composition	Groups of members with mixed poverty composition
Group Characteristics	None	Self-selected small groups of 4-8 people	• Self-selected small subgroups of 5 federated into larger "center" of 20 to 40 people • Required attendance at weekly meetings	• Self-selected groups of 15 to 50 people • Democratic control • Administrative self-sufficiency • Independence • Regular meetings	• Self-selected groups of 15 to 50 people. • Democratic control • Administrative self-sufficiency • Independence	• Self-selected groups of 15 to 200 or more people • Democratic control • Administrative self-sufficiency • Independence • Autonomy in member selection • Regular meetings • Formation of federations of groups
Role of Groups	None	• Approve members • Approve loans	• Approve members • Approve loans • Social support desired	• Groups establish by-laws and policies • Approve, disburse and collect loans	• Groups establish by-laws and policies • Collect, own, and manage savings • Approve, disburse and collect loans	• Groups establish by-laws and policies • Collect, own, and manage savings • Approve, disburse and collect loans
Credit Officer Relationship to Client	Very close relationship with individualized attention	Relatively close	Relatively distant	Distant	Distant	No outside credit officer
Loan Appraisal	Based on careful business viability analysis	Based on minimal business viability analysis	Group involved in loan appraisal	• Group loans processed by agent • Individual loans analyzed by group	• Group loans processed by agent • Individual loans analyzed by group	• No outside loans to group • Individual loans to members analyzed by group

Table 2 continued

Principles	Individual Lending	Latin American Solidarity Group Lending	Grameen Banking	Village Banking	Community-Managed Revolving Loan Fund	Savings and Credit Cooperative/Credit Union
Loan Characteristics	Loans adapted to client needs	• Limited range of loan conditions • Quick processing of follow-up loans	• Limited range of loan conditions • Rotating access to credit • Various types of loans	• Group loan is aggregate of individual loans • Loans disbursed in cycles • Rigid loan conditions	• Group loan based on group equity • Flexible loan conditions to individuals in group	• No outside loans to group • Varied loan amounts available to individual members
Guarantee Mechanisms	Collateral and/or cosigners	Mutual guarantee of all loans	• Mutual guarantee of all loans • Emergency and other savings funds	• Peer pressure from group • Group savings a partial guarantee • No guarantees on individual loans	• Peer pressure from group • Guarantees on individual loans at group discretion	Guarantees on individual loans at discretion of group, often based on savings and/or collateral
Savings Policies	Savings is often not essential	Savings often key to methodology	Savings is mandatory part of methodology	• Savings is essential part of methodology • Loan size based on savings	Savings often required	Savings is the fundamental principle of the methodology
Other Development Services	Business training available for fees, often through partnering organizations	Limited business training, provided either through MED program or partners	• Sometimes an education package based on "16 Decisions" • Training on basics of MED program • Minimal business training	• Training on basics of MED program • Sometimes health education or literacy training	Training on basics of program	Training at discretion of group.

Modified from Waterfield and Duval (1996)

Table 3: Implications of Key Variables in Promotion, Partnering and Provision Models

Assessment Issues	Partnering – Linkage with Savings and Credit Organization / MFI	Promotion – Savings Group or Credit Union	Provision of MED / Microfinance for the poor
Description of Model	A local church or group links with an already existing MED program that will provide the microfinance services, such as a cooperative, MFI, bank, NGO, etc. Requires that the already existing MED program be credible to local group, church.	Facilitating a group to form its own savings club with potential for loans to members. Credit union model in some cases.	Establishing and operating a finance program for the people. Borrowers are "clients." Generally seeks partners for other non-financial development initiatives.
1. Time Horizon: Commitment by Christian Workers and Funding			
1-5 years	Possible.	Possible. Groups may dissolve and reform.	Avoid.
6-10 years	Possible.	Possible. Groups may dissolve and reform.	Possible.
11+ years	Possible.	Possible. Groups may dissolve and reform.	Possible.
2. Sustainability Vision			
Long-term outside subsidy for Christian workers / promoters	Linkage with MFI should no longer require subsidy for finance activities after start-up phase. Subsidies for other developments are valid. The non-finance activities are probably not damaging, but depends on context.	Eventually all finance activities much be self-financed by the savings group, and volunteer driven. Subsidy for other activities probably not damaging, but depends on context.	Extremely difficult to implement, and potentially destructive to local credit culture if microfinance provider relies on outside subsidy over the medium and long-term. Risk of closure is too high.
Short-term outside subsidy for Christian workers / promoters	Possible in finance activities at start-up if savings activities lead.	Subsidy for outside promoter okay at start-up.	Difficult to implement and potentially destructive if there are no clear targets to eliminate subsidies.
Full cost recovery from borrowers / members	Necessary for MFI / finance organization.	Necessary for local savings club / credit union finance activities.	Requires becoming a bank for the poor to provide long-term financial services.

Table 3 continued

3. Services to be Directly Provided by the MED Program		
Microfinance	MFI / finance organization must be credible and acceptable to group, community, church, etc.	Crucial component.	Most providers still focus heavily on the delivery of capital.
Business development training	Possible if MFI / finance organization will not oppose or prohibit it. May require link with another training organization.	Possible. May require link with another training organization.	Possible if limited. Avoid high expenses since clients cannot pay full costs. Seek linkages.
Development training and interventions (health, literacy, etc.)	Possible. Depends partly on vision of MFI / finance organization. May require link with another training organization.	Possible. May require link with another training organization.	Possible if limited. Health training and microfinance are good complements.
Biblical worldview, evangelism, discipleship.	Possible if MFI / finance organization will not oppose it. Difficult if MFI or MFI staff are not credible to local community church. Linkages with other organizations helpful.	Possible. Linkages with other organizations can be helpful.	Possible if limited. Will need a long-term curriculum that requires minimal time. Seek linkages where possible.
Combination of different services provided by MED program.	Possible. Depends partly on vision of MFI / finance organization and whether they will oppose other services. Linkages with another organizations helpful.	Possible. Linkages with other organizations can be helpful.	Combinations of microfinance plus one other are okay. More than that may be difficult due to cost pressures. Seek linkages.
4. Goal for Outreach		
Up to 500	Possible, especially for village banking and other group lending organizations.	Possible. Learn appropriate size limits for savings clubs / credit unions.	Not recommended. Will not reach economies of scale.
501-2,000	Possible with replication.	Possible with replication. Learn size limits for clubs / credit unions.	Difficult to sustain. Uncertain economies of scale.
2,001+	Possible, perhaps difficult, with replication.	Possible, perhaps difficult, with replication.	Possible. Can reach initial economies of scale.

Table 3 continued next page

Table 3 continued

5. Linkages for Services and Technical Help on Financial Services			
Links with MED promoters	Necessary if church does not have skills to negotiate linkage.	Very important for technical assistance.	Not extremely helpful for providers, but can help build bridges.
Links with local MED providers (MFIs, ooops, etc.)	Required part of the model.	Credit union approach requires link with oversight body.	Helpful, see box immediately below…
Links with skilled professionals that can help out on MED / MFI needs.	Can be helpful.	Can help develop basic systems. Credit union networks often provide it.	Basic MIS, accounting, management, etc. necessary if not available in-house.
6. Macroeconomic and Political Conditions			
Inflation rate prevents savings.	Impossible.	Impossible.	Impossible.
Inflation very high but clients still save.	Same as MED provision model.	Let clients set the terms and rates. Interest rates will be high and terms often short.	Interest rates and fees can be very high. Interest rates must be high enough to cover inflation plus operating and financial costs. Rates and loan terms should be structured to give MFI flexibility to raise and lower when necessary.
Political and economic corruption very high.	Same as MED provision model.	Savings clubs / credit unions should have sufficient democratic space to have some ability to hide from and / or resist corruption.	MED provider must have adequate "protection" from corruption demands of external elites. The ethical high road rejects bribery.

Note: Current as of May 1999

Table 4: Summary Table of Cases Researched

MED Program	Country	Year MED Services Began	# Clients	Portfolio (US$)	Microfinance Methodologies Used	Affiliations / Network Membership
Center for Promotion of Andean Development (AYNI)	Peru	1993	189	$34,133	Solidarity Group, Individual Lending, Community Enterprise Lending	Funded by World Relief, no technical support
World Relief/ Cambodia (WR/C)	Cambodia	1992	13,142	$626,259	Village Banking, Individual Lending	World Relief affiliate
Center for Community Transformation (CCT)	Philippines	1994		$300,938	Village Banking	Opportunity International Network member
Fondo de Inversiones Para el Dasarillo de la Micoepresa (FIME)	Dominican Republic	1994	4,129	$1,045,651	Village Banking, Solidarity Group lending, Individual lending	Program of World Vision International
Local Enterprise Assistance Program (LEAP)	Liberia	1995	2,098	$109,221	Village Banking	World Relief affiliate
Project Love in Family Environment (L.I.F.E.)	Thailand	1996	111	$15,567	Individual Lending for agricultural production	YWAM missionary
Sinapi Aba Trust (SAT)	Ghana	1994	8,325	$844,641	Village Banking, Individual lending, some Solidarity Group lending	Opportunity International Network member
Ventures and Entrepreneurship and Development Center in the Orient (VEDCOR)	Manila, Philippines	1993	792	$14,454	Savings and Credit Cooperative capitalized purely by members' savings	None. Desire to create VEDCOR network for member cooperatives

Note: Current as of December 1998

Table 5: Lending Methologies Used by Cases

Christian MED Program	MED Methodologies Used	Comparison to Secular Methodological Standard
AYNI (Peru)	Individual Lending, New Community Enterprise Lending Program	• Individual Lending and poor repayment • Community Enterprise Lending not recommended by secular standards
World Relief Cambodia	Village Banking, New Individual Lending Program	• Village Banking had high repayment and included health training - consistent with "Credit with Education" methodologies of industry. Health training adds delivery cost. • Individual Lending new
Center for Community Transformation (CCT) (Philippines)	Village Banking	Fairly high arrears rate. Fairly high cost structure because of transformation activities.
FIME (Dominican Republic)	Village Banking, Solidarity Group Lending, Individual Lending	• Village Banking fairly standard. Repayment impacted by hurricane in 1997. • Solidarity Group Lending a tool for building Village Banks rather than a graduation target for Village Bank members.
LEAP (Liberia)	Village Banking	• High quality impacted by civil war.
Project L.I.F.E. (Thailand)	Individual Lending	• High cost per borrower with continued high subsidy provided by expatriate - not a standard MED practice.
SAT (Ghana)	Village Banking, Solidarity Group Lending, Individual Lending	• Village Banking high quality • Individual Lending arrears relatively high at 7%
VEDCOR/Goshen Multi-Purpose Cooperative (Philippines)	Savings and Credit Cooperative	Fairly high arrears rate in Goshen partly caused by Asian economic crisis. No network affiliation or oversight as recommended in credit union model for coops of its size.

Note: Current as of May 1999

Table 6: Financial Performance of Christian MED Cases

MED Program	Portfolio at Risk Rates	Adequate Capital Base	Subsidies & Self-Sufficiency Ratios	Program Efficiency	Interest Rates	Leveraging and Borrowed Funds
Secular Standards	• 90 day Portfolio at Risk < 1% • 30 day Portfolio at risk <5%	Reasonable prospects of getting sufficient funding to build loan portfolio to reach operational and financial self-sufficiency. Need to grow capital base.	• Operational self-sufficiency >100% • Full financial self-sufficiency after 5-7 years	• Clients/loan office: 200-400 • Portfolio/loan officer: Depends on context. • Cost/$ loan portfolio: 12-25 cents	• Depends on inflation. • Generally 36%or higher annual flat rate.	Rely on borrowed funds and investors to meet loan capital expansion needs.
AYNI (Peru)	30 day: 75%	Decapitalizing rapidly	• Operational self-sufficiency: 15-20% • Financial self-sufficiency unavailable	• Clients/loan officer: 95 • Portfolio/loan officer: $9,418 • Costs/$ loaned: 1.89	36%declining balance	None
WR/C (Cambodia)	30 day: 4%	Adequate but slowed down growth at several times.	• Operational self-sufficiency: 85% approx. • Financial self-sufficiency: 65% approx.	• Clients/loan officer: 173 • Portfolio/loan officer: $8,240	48-60%flat	None
CCT (Philippines)	90 day: 50% (resolved in 1999)	Not available	Not available	Not available	Not available	None
FIME (Dominican Republic)	Not available	• Adequate for reaching operational self-sufficiency. • Looking to borrow funds to grow.	• Operational self-sufficiency: 103% • Financial self-sufficiency pending.	• Clients/loan officer: 458 • Portfolio/loan officer: $130,706	36%flat plus 2-6% fees.	Currently seeking borrowed funds to expand.

Table 6 continued next page

Table 6 continued

MED Program	Portfolio at Risk Rates	Adequate Capital Base	Subsidies & Self-Sufficiency Ratios	Program Efficiency	Interest Rates	Leveraging and Borrowed Funds
LEAP (Liberia)	30 day: 12%	• Adequate capital to grow at reasonable rate. • Inadequate capital to reach operational self-sufficiency.	• Operational self-sufficiency: 71% • Financial self-sufficiency: 62%	• Clients/loan officer: 175 • Portfolio/loan officer: $9,101	48%flat	None
Project L.I.F.E. (Thailand)	30 day: 21.7%	External donations. Adequate so far.	Not sufficient data	• Clients/field staff: 55 • Portfolio/field staff: $7,783	18%flat	None
SAT (Ghana)	30 day: 0%	Adequate funding.	• Operational self-sufficiency: 122% • Financial self-sufficiency: 88%	• 384 clients/loan officer • Portfolio/loan officer: $32,768	35%flat plus 3% processing fee plus $1.20 other fees.	None
VEDCOR (Philippines)	Unknown but assumed to be very high at GMPC coop.	Local cooperatives capitalized by savings of members.	• VEDCOR costs covered by subsidy from church. • GMPC coop heavily subsidized by church investment income.	Credit coop model. GMPC has one worker and 792 members.	24%flat plus 2% service charge	None. GMPC had previous soft loan from government that was fully repaid on-time.

Note: Current as of December 1998

Table 7: Leadership and Governance in Christian MED Cases

MED Program	Mature Christian Leadership	Governance: Vision-driven & Focused	Indigenous, Trained & Competent	Continuity of Leadership	Ability to Learn, Change, & Adapt
Secular Standards	Religious background not important. Technical management abilities crucial.	Competent board of directors that helps meet legal obligations, provides strategic direction, fiduciary guidance, oversight to the program, and assesses and renews itself over time. Balances the social and profit objectives.	Nationals at CEO, management and field level. All staff trained in corporate culture (including vision) and operating procedures, primarily on the job. Competent leadership has combination of social commitment and management skills and motivates staff.	Visionary leadership often needed to start MED program. With scale comes need for professional management. Strong MFIs have often had one leader that has been able to grow throughout their history.	Up-to-date on best practices of MED world. Intimate knowledge of MED program. Able to recognize need for change in program and staff and allow change to happen.
AYNI (Peru)	Evangelical director. Some earlier field staff not Christian.	Peruvian board of directors has no members with MED experience. Has had varied visions throughout history.	National management. Lack qualified accountant/ bookkeeper.	Director also founder. All other staff very recent hires.	Not well connected to 'best practices." Responses to 1997 repayment problems were rapid. Current community enterprise MED not sound practice.
WR/C (Cambodia)	Evangelical Cambodian CEO. All management Christian. Some field staff Buddhists but most become Christians.	Expatriate board of directors with significant NGO experience.	National management. Expatriate advisor. Previously expatriate management. Finding educated Cambodian Christians is very difficult.	Nationals in management in WR/C for many years. Process of building up leadership in Cambodia long-term and difficult.	Responded well to 1996 repayment crisis. New loan products.
CCT (Philippines)	Evangelical management and staff.	Filipino board of directors with strong Christian backgrounds. Vision is largely for Kingdom Building using microenterprise as an entry point.	National leadership from inception.	Founder remains director	Experimentation on methods and hands-on research and development.

Table 7 continued next page

Table 7 continued

MED Program	Mature Christian Leadership	Governance: Vision-driven & Focused	Indigenous, Trained & Competent	Continuity of Leadership	Ability to Learn, Change, & Adapt
FIME (Dominican Republic)	Evangelical management and most of staff evangelical.	A local MED program of World Vision DR. Linked to WV/DR agendas, sites and child sponsorship programs and this has caused struggles with some failed loan products.	National leadership from inception.	2 directors. Previous director now head of WV/DR.	Multiple loan products that respond to different contexts. Survived 1997 hurricane.
LEAP (Liberia)	Evangelical management and staff.	LEAP a program of Access – relief and development arm of the Association of Evangelicals of Liberia. No oversight by board members with MED interest or expertise.	Liberian CEO with banking experience.	Founder is still director in spite of 1997 civil war.	Was able to survive 1997 civil war and rebuild. Experimenting with $ loans now.
Project L.I.F.E. (Thailand)	YWAM missionaries have headed project. Staff are Christians.	5 member advisory committee guides funds use. Foreign-controlled Foundation controls organization. Desire to eventually nationalize ownership of MED program	Missionaries have run organization since start-up. Nationals do administrative and technical work under guidance and training of missionary.	YWAM missionaries have headed project. Some vulnerability in case they have to leave unexpectedly. Who will run the program then?	Linked with church-based funeral fund.
SAT (Ghana)	Evangelical leadership and staff.	Evangelicals on board. Very committed and active in oversight.	National leadership with very qualified CEO.	First CEO committed fraud. Board stepped in, provided continuity, hired 2nd CEO and watches closely.	Adopting village banking, evaluates its work.
VEDCOR (Philippines)	Evangelicals that are hired by local church.	Evangelical individuals and organizations on VEDCOR board. Local coop boards have varying degrees of vision and focus, some of which are not conducive to strong microfinance services.	No expatriate involvement in start-up or management of VEDCOR or coops.	VEDCOR has continuity of leadership. Coops vary	VEDCOR knows "sound practices" of MED. Coops vary.

Note: Current as of May 1999

Table 8: Spiritual Transformation in Christian MED Cases

MED Program	Spiritual Equipping of Staff	Spiritual Ministries to Clients	Building up Local Churches	Incentives for Spiritual Ministries	Indicators for Spiritual Ministries
Secular Standards	None	None	None	None	None
AYNI (Peru)	Weekly devotions. No training on integrating spiritual ministries into staff daily work	Staff do individual ministry. Some clients have become Christians. Pre-evangelism as Roman Catholics see integrity of Christian program.	Targets Presbyterian churches and has their prayer support. Mixed results. Some tithes up. One loan officer is pastor and has had declining attendance. Some churches have better understanding of "living out" the gospel now.	None yet.	None yet.
WR/C (Cambodia)	Weekly devotions led by staff. Staff rotate leading devotions so that they learn how. No current training on integrating spiritual ministries.	Staff do individual ministry. Some clients have become Christians. Pre-evangelism through identification as Christian program and working with integrity. Program partners with World Relief with child health evangelism so that areas are covered by both.	Some house churches started as result of staff ministry and partnership with child health evangelism ministry. No direct work with churches because of feeling that churches are weak. One church-based village bank in capital city.	Staff lead weekly devotions and get skills in leading Bible studies.	Case studies gathered periodically by World Relief staff. No other indicators used locally yet.
CCT (Philippines)	Not available	Staff do individual ministry. Some clients have become Christians. CCT links with other Philippine ministries for evangelism and	Mixed. Links with churches not from area for evangelism & discipleship.	Not available	Not available
FIME (Dominican Republic)	Devotions and counseling with staff. Developing plan for discipling staff.	Staff do individual ministry (one is pastor). Witnessing to non-believers by Christians in village banks. Seek to systematize experience of model village banks. Developing Bible studies for village banks.	Efforts depend on loan officer. Some church women's groups have village banks linked with FIME Willow Creek Association, funded a chaplain for FIME who seeks to train churches in holistic ministry.	Director wrote up cases where program impacted local churches. Distributed to FIME and World Vision. Pastor on staff to emphasize spiritual ministries. Is creating a database of client transformation that it seeks to publish	Collects testimonies to help church-based village banks develop targets.

Table 8 continued next page

Table 8 continued

MED Program	Spiritual Equipping of Staff	Spiritual Ministries to Clients	Building up Local Churches	Incentives for Spiritual Ministries	Indicators for Spiritual Ministries
LEAP (Liberia)	Extensive training in ministry skills of human relations, relational evangelism, & Biblical counseling. Mentoring of staff by CEO. Daily staff devotions led by staff on rotating basis.	Staff pray with clients. Staff encourage village banks to elect a chaplain. Weekly devotions in village banks coordinated by each village bank's chaplain. Tribal reconciliation through Bible teaching and multi-tribal banks.	Most village banks based in evangelical churches but with a right balance of church involvement. Pastors not implementers. LEAP staff encourage pastors to use village banking as outreach tool. Most village bank meetings held in or near churches. A few pastors have mismanaged village bank funds.	Leadership by example of CEO. CEO loves prayer and praise. Great personal depth and Bible knowledge by CEO. Only hire spiritually-minded believers. Being a program of Association of Evangelicals of Liberia keeps spiritual focus.	Some anecdotal stories of people that have become Christians.
Project L.I.F.E. (Thailand)	Weekly devotions with staff.	Some clients have become Christians and have overcome alcoholism. Pre-evangelism by program.	Works alongside local church. Church unofficial advisor. Missionary meets with pastor weekly to maintain good relationship. Church has funeral fund that MED program requires clients to belong to.	Part time work allows 2 staff to be involved in church activities.	None identified.
SAT (Ghana)	Daily staff devotions.	High spiritual impact. Biblically-based MED training modules for clients. Teaching in village bank meetings. Pre-evangelism to Muslims through honesty and integrity.	21 of 105 village banks linked to churches. Partnerships with Luke Society, Prison Fellowship (Geo Trust), and TechnoServe (staffed mainly by Christians)	1997 Transformation study. Staff see jobs as "callings" or "ministries." Opportunity International Network now requires kingdom building activities to be in business plans and budgets of all network members.	1997 external transformation study used following indicators: • financial support for church activities • participation in church activities • church attendance • prayer/devotional life
VEDCOR (Philippines)	Workers and volunteers trained in friendship evangelism, cell group leadership.	Friendship evangelism by all staff and volunteers.	VEDCOR trains churches to implement saving & credit cooperatives. Churches build "financial center" groups into cell groups. One pastor has mismanaged cooperative funds.	None documented. Church-based MED.	None documented. Church-based MED.

Note: Current as of May 1999

Table 9: Other Strategic Issues

MED Program	Fits with Context	Partnership and Networks	Fraud Control	MIS and other Systems	Assessing Impact	Repayment Crises
Secular Standards	Must fit closely with economic, demographic, cultural characteristics of people and communities. Economic environment, markets, infrastructure, government policies also important.	Important for furthering the program's vision, staff development, better service for clients, referrals to other organizations, access to funds.	Crucial. Use code of conduct, transparency, multiple cross-checks, adequate salaries and benefits for employees to lessen need for fraud, regular supervision	Accurate and timely portfolio reports crucial for all programs, especially those upscaling. Need portfolio reports, balance sheet, income statement, and cash flow statements at least on monthly basis.	Expensive and very difficult. Repayment is main indicator of positive impact.	Expect them. Admit and attack them.
AYNI (Peru)	Very difficult context – Shining Path area. FINCA does well in that area though.	Partners with World Vision Peru and has gained knowledge. Needs to join a MED network to educate and keep it accountable.	No cases of fraud	Poor MIS. Bookkeeper has no MED experience.	Anecdotes	1997 crisis. Responded by closing branch and writing off loans.
WR/C (Cambodia)	Careful fit with religious, government, and donor context. Competition with minimalist MFI.	Beginning partnerships with missions in Cambodia. Member of World Relief MED network. Received technical support, funds.	Fraud case in 1996 helped stimulate repayment crisis.	MIS was poor before repayment crisis. Now more effective.	Serious effort. Used early indicators developed by AIMS (USAID) at individual and group level. Also did health monitoring of children over time.	1996-97. Multiple reasons: flooding, fraud, death of 2 field staff all at same time, overrapid growth with poor portfolio quality, poor MIS, etc. Responses: admit it, get help, attack it.
CCT (Philippines)	Not available	Member of APPEND national MED network and Opportunity Network. Received funds, technical support.	Not available	Not available	Not available	1998-99 repayment crisis resolved by writing off some loans, adopted ASA methodology.
FIME (Dominican Republic)	Experimenting with different methodologies. Using churches in different ways.	Works with Willow Creek Association in spiritual ministries. Receives MED technical support from WVI MED advisor in US.	No cases reported.	Started with manual system. Developed its own computerized MIS (rather than use one provided by World Vision). This failed when they grew too big. Currently testing 2nd generation computerized system developed locally.	Anecdotes	Have a lawyer on staff now to handle defaults. Hurricane stimulated some loan restructuring and write-offs. Arrears hurt funding access but program recovered.

Table 9 continued next page

Table 9 continued

MED Program	Fits with Context	Partnership and Networks	Fraud Control	MIS and other Systems	Assessing Impact	Repayment Crises
LEAP (Liberia)	Civil war context difficult. Doing tribal reconciliation.	Partners with local churches. Part of Association of Evangelicals of Liberia and World Relief MED network and receive funds and technical support.	No cases reported.	Uses World Relief spreadsheet-based MIS, but personnel not well enough trained until recently.	Anecdotes for promotion. Impact tools waiting for development of better tools in USAID impact studies.	Civil war induced in 1997. Most of loan portfolio collected because clients felt services were valuable.
Project L.I.F.E. (Thailand)	Rural Thailand context. Agriculture-based economy.	Partners with local church and church's funeral fund. No technical MED support.	No cases reported.	Spreadsheet-based system is maintained by missionary. Insufficient variables tracked.	Anecdotes.	No crisis reported.
SAT (Ghana)	Uses Christian population of Ghana effectively. Contextualizing in Muslim areas	Partners with local churches, Luke Society, Prison Fellowship, Technoserve. Member of Opportunity International Network and received technical support, funds from network.	CEO committed fraud in 1996. Board stepped in to save organization.	Uses purchased MIS database. Interested in piloting new MIS being developed by Opportunity International Network.	Transformation study in 1997.	No crisis reported.
VEDCOR (Philippines)	Churches build programs based on their context. Very localized control of financial centers.	VEDCOR provides limited technical support and almost no oversight to coops. Additional oversight might help strengthen coops.	Cases of fraud in church-based coops. One by pastor. Coop structure very decentralized and difficult to oversee	Manual MIS that is okay for smaller coops. Goshen coop too big for current manual system.	Anecdotes	1997 Asian economic crisis has impacted coops. Current poor repayment has stopped most new lending at Goshen coop.

Note: Current as of May 1999

Bibliography

Adams, D.W. & Fitchett, D.A. (1992). *Informal Finance in Low-income countries*. Boulder: Westview Press.

Adams, D.W., D.H. Graham, & J.D. Von Pischke, Editors (1984). *Undermining Rural Development with Cheap Credit.* Boulder: Westview Press.

Ardener, S. & Burman, S. (1995). *Money-go-rounds: The Importance of Rotating Savings and Credit Associations for Women.* Oxford: Berg Publishers Ltd..

Bouman, F.J.A. & Hospes, O. (1994). *Financial Landscapes Reconstructed: The Fine Art of Mapping Development.* Boulder: Westview Press.

Bouman, F.J.A. & Moll, H.A.J. (1992.) Informal Finance in Indonesia. In D. Adams and D. Fitchett (Eds.), *Informal Finance in Low-income Countries* (pp. 209-224). Boulder: Westview Press.

Burbank, K. (1999). *A Christian Perspective on Microenterprise Loans and the Payment of Loan Interest.* Manuscript submitted for publication, Eastern College.

Campion, A. & Frankiewicz, C. (1999). *Guidelines for the Effective Governance of Microfinance Institutions. The Microfinance Network Occassional Paper No. 3.* Microfinance Network. Available: http://www.bellanet.org /partners/mfn/

Carver, J. (1990), *Boards that Make a Difference,* Jossey-Bass Inc., Publishers

Christen, R. P., Rhyne, E., Vogel, R. C., & McKean, C. (1995). *Maximizing the Outreach of Microenterprise Finance: The Emerging Lessons of Successful Programs*. Washington, D.C.: USAID Center for Development Information and Evaluation.

Edgcomb, E. & Cawley, J. Editors. (1993). *An Institutional Guide for Enterprise Development Organizations*. New York: SEEP.

Johnson, S. & Rogaly, B. (1997). *Microfinance and Poverty Reduction*. Oxford: Oxfam UK.

Miller, D. (1998). *Discipling the Nations: The Power of Truth to Transform Culture.* Seattle: YWAM Publications.

Myers, B. (1999) *Walking with the Poor: Principles and Practices of Transformational Development.* Maryknoll: Orbis and World Vision.

Rhyne, E. & Rotblatt, L. S. (1994). *What Makes Them Tick? Exploring the Anatomy of Major Microenterprise Finance Organizations*. Cambridge, MA: ACCION International.

Rock, R., Otero, M. & Saltzman, S. (1998). *Principles and Practices of Microfinance Governance*. Bethesda, MD: Microenterprise Best Practices Project, Development Alternatives, Inc. (On-line). Available: www.dai.com

Rutherford, S. (1999). *The Poor and Their Money: An Essay About Financial Services for Poor People*. Manchester: Institute for Development Policy and Management, University of Manchester (On-Line). 1999. Available: http://www.man.ac.uk/idpm/fdrp_wp3.htm

SEEP Network. (1995). *Financial Ratio Analysis for Micro-finance institu-*

tions. New York: Pact Publications.

Sider, R. (1997). *Rich Christians in an Age of Hunger: Moving from Affluence to Generosity*. Dallas: Word.

Von Pischke, J.D. (1991). *Finance at the Frontier: Debt Capacity and the Role of Credit in the Private Economy*. Washington, D.C.: The World Bank.

Von Pischke, J.D. (1994). *Structuring Credit to Manage Real Risks*. In F.J.A. Bouman & O. Hospes (Eds.), Financial Landscapes Reconstructed: The Fine Art of Mapping Development (pp. 49-70). Boulder: Westview Press.

Waterfield, C. & Duval, A. (1996). *Care Savings and Credit Sourcebook*. Atlanta: CARE.

Waterfield, C. and Ramsing, N. (1998). *Handbook for Management Information Systems for Microfinance Institutions*. Washington, D.C.: CGAP/World Bank.

MED and Development Resources from Christian Authors

Buckley, S. (1998), *Usury Friendly: The Ethics of Moneylending — A Biblical Interpretation*, Grove Books Limited.

Burbank, K. (1999). *A Christian Perspective on Microenterprise Loans and the Payment of Loan Interest.* Manuscript submitted for publication, Eastern College.

Bussau, D. (1998). *Reflections on Christian Microenterprise Development*. Sydney: Opportunity International/Australia.

Bussau, D. & Vinay S. (1998). *How Then Should We Lend? A Biblical validation of microenterprise development*. Sydney: Opportunity International/Australia.

Bussau, D., Beggs, A., Martin, E., (1999), *Board Self-Assessment: A Resource Kit for Facilitators*, The Governance Center, Opportunity International Australia.

Bussau, D., Beggs, A., Martin, E., (1999), *Governing with Policy: A Resource Kit for Facilitators*, The Governance Center, Opportunity International Australia.

Keller, T. J. (1997). *Ministries of mercy: The Call of the Jericho Road*. Phillipsburg, NJ: P & R Publishing Company.

Miller, D. L. & Guthrie, S. (1998). *Discipling Nations: The Power of Truth to Transform Cultures.* Seattle: YWAM Publishing.

Remenyi, J. (1991). *Where credit is due: Income Generating Programmes for the Poor in Developing Countries*. London: Intermediate Technology Publications.

Sider, R. (1997). *Rich Christians in an Age of Hunger: Moving from Affluence to Generosity*. Dallas: Word.

Waterfield, C. & Ramsing, N. (1998). *Handbook for Management Information Systems for Microfinance Institutions*. Washington, D.C.: CGAP/World Bank.

Waterfield, C. & Duval, A. (1996). *Care Savings and Credit Sourcebook*. Atlanta: CARE.

MED Resources on the Internet

Christian Development Organizations Implementing MED

Opportunity International: www.opportunity.org.au
  www.opportunity.org.uk, www.opportunity.org

World Relief: www.wr.org

Food for the Hungry: www.fh.org

World Vision: www.wvi.org

Enterprise Development International: www.endpoverty.org

Mennonite Economic Development Associates www.meda.org

Hope International: www.hopeinternational.net

World Hope International: www.worldhope.org

Farms International: www.farmsinternational.com

Technical MED Resources

- Chalmers Center for Economic Development at Covenant College: www.chalmers.org
- The Virtual Library on Microcredit: www.gdrc.org/icm
- USAID Microenterprise: www.microlinks.org
- The Enterprise Development Website: www.enterweb.org/microcre.htm
- The Small Enterprise Education and Promotion (SEEP) Network: www.seepnetwork.org

- Consultative Group to Assist the Poor (World Bank): www.cgap.org
- UNCDF Microfinance Website: www.uncdf.org/english/ microfinance
- PACT Publications: www.pactpublications.com
- Intermediate Technology Publications: www.itdgpublishing.org.uk
- World Vision Resources: www.worldvisionresources.com
- MARC Publications: www.marcpublications.com
- Credit and Savings for Hard Core Poor (CASHPOR): www.cashpor.org
- (CGAP)'s Microfinance Gateway: www.microfinancegateway.org
- The Microcredit Summit Campaign: www.microcreditsummit.org
- Freedom from Hunger Technical Resource site: www.ffhtechnical.org
- CARE Economic Development & Technical Resource e-library: www.kcenter.com/care/edu
- Christian Transformation Resource Centre: www.ctrc-cmed.org
- Microsave: www.microsave.org
- The Mix (Microfinance Information Exchange): www.themix.org
- FOA Rural Finance Learning Center: Self-Study Lessons: http://www.ruralfinance.org/servlet/CDSServlet?status=ND01NT Y4JjY9ZW4mMzM9KiYzNz1rb3M~
- International Labour Organization (ILO) Business Development Services (BDS) Website:

www.ilo.org/dyn/empent/empent.portal?p_lang=EN&p_prog=S&p_subprog=BD

- Many SME (Small and Medium Enterprise) Development Links, including many BDS websites, can be found at: www.weitzenegger.de/en/links.html